P9-CFP-092

NoMarks

Alfred Hitchcock is one of the few filmmakers to combine a strong reputation for high-art filmmaking with great mass-audience popularity. This introduction to his oeuvre provides an overview of a long and prolific career. David Sterritt examines, among other issues, the varied influences on his work; the themes that run through many of his films; the overlooked importance of his presence within his films, including his famous cameo appearances and the characters who "represent" him within the story; his fascination with performance and the ambiguities of illusion and reality; and the question of viewing the filmmaker and his work through the auteur theory. Also discussed is the relationship between Hitchcock as a serious, even tormented, artist and Hitchcock as a magician with a weakness for cinematic practical jokes. Sterritt then provides in-depth analysis of key Hitchcock films: *Blackmail*, his first talkie; *Shadow of a Doubt*, one of his personal favorites; *The Wrong Man*, which questions the nature of guilt and innocence; *Vertigo*, arguably his most profound work; *Psycho*, his most savage look at the nature of evil; and *The Birds*, his last masterpiece and one of his most widely misunderstood films.

The Films of Alfred Hitchcock

CAMBRIDGE FILM CLASSICS

General Editor: Raymond Carney, Boston University

Other books in the series:

Peter Bondanella, *The Films of Roberto Rossellini*
Sam B. Girgus, *The Films of Woody Allen*
Robert Phillip Kolker and Peter Beicken, *The Films of Wim Wenders*
Scott MacDonald, *Avant-Garde Film*

The Films of
Alfred Hitchcock

DAVID STERRITT

CAMBRIDGE
UNIVERSITY PRESS

Published by the Press Syndicate of the University of Cambridge
The Pitt Building, Trumpington Street, Cambridge CB2 1RP
40 West 20th Street, New York, NY 10011-4211, USA
10 Stamford Road, Oakleigh, Victoria 3166, Australia

© Cambridge University Press 1993

First published 1993

Printed in the United States of America

Library of Congress Cataloging-in-Publication Data
Sterritt, David.
The films of Alfred Hitchcock / David Sterritt.
p. cm. – (Cambridge film classics)
Includes bibliographical references.
ISBN 0-521-39133-4. – ISBN 0-521-39814-2 (pbk.)
1. Hitchcock, Alfred, 1899–1980 – Criticism and interpretation.
I. Title. II. Series.
PN1998.3.H58S74 1993
791.43'0233'092–dc20 92–25768
CIP

A catalog record for this book is available from the British Library.

ISBN 0-521-39133-4 hardback
ISBN 0-521-39814-2 paperback

To Ginnie

Contents

I

Introduction

Alfred Hitchcock is among the few directors to combine a strong reputation for high-art filmmaking — even his detractors grant the consistency and technical ingenuity of his work — with enormous mass-audience popularity. The broadly based interest in Hitchcock's work stems from a number of factors, including his lifelong fascination with one of the fundamental concerns of modern art: the tension between order and chaos. It is clear from his key works (as well as from his biography) that he perceived this tension not just abstractly or intellectually, but as a visceral concern — he was in a subliminal but perpetual panic over it. This helps explain the perceptual and emotional properties of his films. It also sheds light on the obsessive control he exercised over them, from his compulsively precise camera and editing styles to his "cattledriver" attitude toward performers and his fixation on vision as the ultimate arbiter of communication and reality itself.

Hitchcock expresses his deep-seated fear of encroaching chaos in various ways. He inflicts vulnerability on his characters by shifting the relationships between reality and illusion, often in settings that allude to stages or theaters; he places characters in confining environments that connote suffocation and paralysis rather than safety or security; he represses key thematic material too dangerous or forbidden to be actualized, thus creating a kind of "shadow film" that colors and modifies everything we see and hear. Such observations lead us to the culminating fact of Hitchcock's universe: the transcendence of physical conflict over psychological and even moral confrontation with evil.

Studies often miss the complexity of Hitchcock's achievement by leaning too far toward either thematic analysis — examining his scenarios and story lines more intently than the films as cinematic experiences — or technical analysis that sheds light on isolated corners without illuminating the canon, or even the individual film, as a whole. Since the cinema specialist and the everyday moviegoer share an interest in Hitchcock's work, he is an ideal subject for analysis that attempts to seek out the relationships among his technical, stylistic, and thematic strategies; to examine these in broadly cinematic terms; and to conjoin them with the dramatic, humanistic, and even spiritual resonances that characterize his best films.

In the years since auteur analysis lost its dominating position on the American film-studies landscape, it has become commonplace for books about "The Films of So-and-So" to include disclaimers, excuses, and explanations of what the writer *really means* when So-and-So's name is mentioned. True to that spirit, when I say Alfred Hitchcock in these pages I don't mean only the odd-looking individual (a "symphony of circles," one journalist called him) who sat in the director's chair for 53 productions, also popping briefly into camera range in most of them. I also mean the phalanx of collaborators (some regular, some occasional, some one-shots) who contributed major and minor ingredients to all his works. Beyond this, I mean the great complex of social, political, economic, and psychological forces that influenced all these people in uncountable ways.

And yet, and yet. While all this is true and important, it is not certain that auteurism has lost its value (or revealed a lack of value that was present all along) as definitively as some critics and scholars have insisted. As a means of organizing film history – especially American film history – it has proven its utility; as a means of emphasizing and exploring the human dimension of moviemaking – especially in the potentially dehumanizing environment of the studio system – it has proved invaluable, at least in the hands of its more thoughtful practitioners.

Hitchcock, moreover, is a special case. Although he never wrote his own screenplays, as did such peers as Orson Welles and Preston Sturges, he exercised great care in shaping the screenplays that others wrote for him. He was able to do this because of the extraordinary degree of personal power he gained in the film industry by virtue of, among other factors, the box-office success of his movies and the public-relations value of his personal appearances in cameo roles, advertising campaigns, and TV programs. He used this power, abetted by his strong technical facility, to control every aspect of his films, from preproduction planning to opening-day publicity. As much as any major filmmaker ever has, he channeled the talent of his collaborators and the temper of his times into coherent narrative/aesthetic patterns dictated by his own deepest instincts.

The origin of Hitchcock's exceptional ability is not clear. He did not, for example, come from an artistically inclined family background as Welles and Sturges did. Born in 1899 in London, he grew up in a middle-class merchant household; a central incident of his childhood, according to an anecdote he never tired of repeating, was a momentary taste of jail arranged by his father and a local policeman, as punishment for some small misbehavior. After attending a Jesuit college, he entered the film industry at age 21 as a writer and illustrator of silent-movie title cards. He worked his way up to such positions as art director and production manager, making his directorial debut with *The Pleasure Garden,* released in 1927. The previous year he had married his assistant, Alma Reville, who continued to be an important (but low-profile) collaborator throughout his career. The first true "Hitchcock film," the celebrated thriller *The Lodger: A Story of the London Fog,* came soon after his marriage; his first sound production, *Blackmail,* was released in 1929. His first American film, *Rebecca,* won the Academy Award for best picture of 1940. He died in 1980 while preparing what would have been his 54th feature.

There are few clues in the Hitchcock chronology to indicate whence his inspirations came or why they developed as they did. It becomes all the more necessary, therefore, to identify and assess the transpersonal forces that made themselves felt in his work despite his passion for personal control – or, as an antiauteurist might skeptically say, the illusion of such control. Since his thematic and stylistic preoccupations remained remarkably stable throughout the decades of his career, one might begin such an investigation by examining his formative years in the British film industry, remembering that the industry was itself in a formative and immature stage during the 1920s and 1930s. Tom Ryall has singled out a number of forces that influenced British film culture at this time.[1] Among them are the following:

the international popularity of mainstream Hollywood cinema;
the existence of an alternative "Film Society" movement in England;
the intellectual prestige of documentary film;
interest in Soviet montage theory;
interest in German expressionist filmmaking; and
the popularity of crime and sex in British popular culture.

Filmmakers who were subject to this convergence of forces tended to make fairly definite choices among alternatives suggested by the first three items. Naturally there was a strong temptation to make movies in imitation of Hollywood, aiming at success not only with British audiences – who were conditioned, and happily so, to Hollywood productions – but also

3

with American audiences, even though this goal generally proved unattainable. It is obvious to anyone familiar with Hitchcock's subsequent career that he was far from averse to many of the themes and stylistics long associated with American filmmaking. If popular success and a comfortable career had been his only aspirations, he might well have clung to the Hollywood model, becoming an accomplished professional storyteller and perhaps little more.

Hitchcock possessed a broad streak of artistic as well as box-office ambition, however. He was impressed by unconventional styles more easily found in film-society showings than on commercial screens, and by the very un-Hollywood stylistic ideas he encountered during a brief period of work at UFA, the great German studio. He must also have been aware that many film intellectuals of the 1920s and 1930s were being drawn away from "entertainment" movies by the notion of an "art" cinema based on documentary principles.

Hitchcock did not follow any of these leads to the extent of abandoning mainstream film production; yet each left a lasting mark on the young director. *The Lodger,* for example, joins a conventional thriller plot and gothic characterizations to a shadowy mise-en-scène with strong Germanic overtones, and to an editing style influenced by Sergei Eisenstein as well as D. W. Griffith and other American pioneers. And whether or not Hitchcock was familiar with Soviet theories on the importance of sound–image counterpoint in talkies, *Blackmail* – surely the greatest of his 1920s films – shows a strong awareness that disjuncture can help prevent the tyranny of word over image, and vice versa.

The complexity of Hitchcock's interaction with the film aesthetics of this period, and the lasting impression this interaction made on him, can be illustrated by his relationship with documentary cinema. Many of his British productions – such as *The Lodger, The Ring, The Manxman,* and *Blackmail* – contain strong documentary elements, especially (as Ryall notes) in the opening sequences, which establish fundamental aspects of the world imagined by each film. In part, this reflects Hitchcock's interest in the documentary "art film" movement headed by John Grierson and others. It also reflects Hitchcock's rapport with a general tendency, felt most strongly in the 1930s, to put more faith in documentary than in pure fiction – a tendency encouraged by diversifying uses of the camera, which James Agee called "the central instrument of our time" in 1936. "The camera is a prime symbol of the thirties' mind . . . less because the mind was endlessly fragmented," writes William Stott, "than because the mind aspired to the quality of authenticity, of direct and immediate experience, that the camera captures

4

in all it photographs."² This sense of "authenticity" keenly interested Hitchcock.

So did the challenge of capturing a kind of reality not usually found in British movies. Conventional films, as a 1937 article in *World Film News* complained, generally pictured 1930s Britain as "a nation of retired businessmen, mill owners, radio singers, actors, detectives, newspapermen, leading ladies, soldiers, secret servicemen, crooks, smugglers and international jewel thieves" rather than people with everyday jobs and ordinary problems.³ By contrast, homes and businesses in Hitchcock's early works are often filmed with an attention to gritty, workaday details calculated to offset the more flamboyant portrait of England frequently manifested in mainstream pictures. Lindsay Anderson notes such examples as the restaurant and tobacconist's shop in *Blackmail*, the chapel in *The Man Who Knew Too Much* (1934), the country house in *The 39 Steps* (1935), the movie theater in *Sabotage* (1936).⁴

Hitchcock acknowledged, in a 1937 article for *Kine Weekly*, that he was consciously trying to put what he called "that vital central stratum of British humanity, the middle class" onto the screen, adding that he hoped "we shall do unto America what they have done unto us, and make the cheerful man and girl of our middle class as colourful and dramatic to them as their ordinary everyday citizens are to the audiences of England."⁵ (In the same year, however, he admitted the difficulty of making English subjects appealing to the English themselves: "One difficulty...is that English audiences seem to take more interest in American life – I suppose because it has a novelty value. They are rather easily bored by everyday scenes in their own country."⁶)

In addition to stating one of his early priorities, Hitchcock's comment on "that vital central stratum" anticipates a strategy that would become one of his chief trademarks: the penchant for showing violence and chaos not only in violent and chaotic settings, but often in ordinary places (frequently pleasant, sunny, crowded) where they beset ordinary people as they go about their ordinary business. Although his later works employ stylized elements at times – *The Birds*, say, and *Marnie* – the tendency toward surface realism continues to be strongly felt decades after his formative period, even in movies with subjects and ambiences very different from those of Anderson's examples. The look and sensibility of *The Wrong Man* (1956), for instance, are powerfully influenced by documentary traditions. Even such an apparently light and artificial concoction as *To Catch a Thief* (1955) bears traces of Hitchcock's documentary impulse, moreover, here translated into a very different idiom. After a credit sequence that indicates the setting and mood of the story with a shot of a travel-agency window, the largely wordless opening sequence alternates conspicuously acted shots of burglary aftermaths with realistic views of a cat (introducing the narrative's "cat burglar" motif) stalking across real-looking rooftops. Although this is not a documentary sequence, its shop-window and stalking-cat shots are so completely literalized – visually and metaphorically – as to recall Hitchcock's roots in the documentary tradition despite the whimsical narrative that follows them.

Other early influences on Hitchcock's work, including Soviet montage theory (associated with Vsevolod Pudovkin, Lev Kuleshov, Eisenstein, and others) and the German expressionist style, also continue to echo in his later films. Pictures related to the 1940s film noir cycle, for example, such as *Shadow of a Doubt* (1943) and *Notorious* (1946), have inflections of lighting and camera angle that recall expressionist techniques; and the editing of many classic sequences – most famously the shower murder in *Psycho* (1960) – is steeped in Eisenstein's notions, as are disjunctions between sound and image in numerous films.

Such stylistic tendencies can be traced across Hitchcock's whole career. Indeed, an understanding of his work must involve recognition of all the forces so far mentioned – classical American film, various national cinemas, documentary expression, popular culture, and so forth – not only in isolation, but also as they interacted with other factors: Hitchcock's artistic ambitions, his wish for praise from high-culture sources, his even stronger wish for mass-audience appeal, his desire to explore social and philosophical issues through visual narrative. And don't forget that key Hitchcockian characteristic, the love of a good (or bad!) practical joke, be it on the people *in* his films or the people *watching* his films. Such diversity recalls the "dialogic" principle of literary theorist M. M. Bakhtin, according to which "everything means, is understood, as a part of a greater whole – there is a constant interaction between meanings, all of which have the potential of conditioning others."[7] Such a dynamic is clearly at work in Hitchcock's British films and continues to operate even more richly – complicated by new production and marketing considerations that Hitchcock encountered after his move to Hollywood – in his later work.

One means of sifting through so many contributory elements in Hitchcock's work, as in the work of other significant filmmakers, has been the auteurist practice of seeking consistent themes, preoccupations, and (that favorite auteurist term) "obsessions" running through his canon. This methodology gained its first major foothold in Hitchcock studies when Eric Rohmer and Claude Chabrol published their groundbreaking book *Hitchcock: The First Forty-Four Films* in 1957, suggesting a compact list of main

Hitchcockian themes and emphasizing the religious elements – specifically Roman Catholic attitudes and outlooks – that they found pervading (and even determining) the films. Many later critics have worked along roughly similar lines, finding concentrations of thematic and "obsessional" material to explain, justify, or consolidate their own interpretations of the on-screen evidence. Key themes to emerge from such studies include:

the ambiguity of guilt and innocence;
the transference of guilt from one individual to another;
the fascination with a guilty woman;
the therapeutic function of obsession and vulnerability; and
the equation of knowledge and danger.

These points do not exhaust the list of major thematic concerns, by any means. Others are also important, from the "confession" theme posited by Rohmer and Chabrol to "fear of the devouring, voracious mother," in Tania Modleski's phrase.[8] Each of those listed above may claim a persistent and resonant presence in Hitchcock's oeuvre over a period of decades, however, and thus deserves a brief overview before any deeper examination of individual films.

The first two points are closely intertwined. On its most transparent level, the ambiguity theme can simply mean that guilty people look innocent (Uncle Charlie in *Shadow of a Doubt*) and vice versa (Hannay in *The 39 Steps*). More interestingly, a genuine moral ambiguity may inhere in a character's decisions and behaviors: In both versions of *The Man Who Knew Too Much* (1934/1956), for instance, the female protagonist knows that action on her part could result in harm to her kidnapped child, and hence – despite her seemingly justified self-image as a decent and gentle person – finds herself (almost) allowing a murder to proceed.

Moral ambiguity crops up consistently in the transfer-of-guilt motif, which takes many forms in many films, but rests ultimately on the ambiguity of guilt itself. The mysterious visitor of *The Lodger* is mistaken for a murderer *he* wants to destroy; the policeman of *Blackmail* precipitates a death by hiding his girlfriend's responsibility for a killing; the priest of *I Confess* cannot refute a false accusation of murder; the heroes of *The 39 Steps* and *North by Northwest* are hunted for murders committed by others; the protagonist of *Vertigo* remains ignorant of his part in a murder scheme while wrongly believing that he failed to prevent a suicide; a belligerent man is branded a murderer in *Frenzy* while the amiable culprit goes unsuspected; and so forth. Guilt may also be "transferred" within a single human psyche, as when the protagonists of *Spellbound* and *Marnie* become the victims of their own overactive superegos because of deaths for which they are physically, but not morally responsible.

Actual guilt also plays a part in Hitchcock's cinema, of course, and while this often attaches itself to men, there does seem to be a preponderance of interest in the female variety. Hitchcock's approach to the guilt and innocence of women is diversified. The female protagonists of *Blackmail* and *Under Capricorn* seem to have been justified in committing their "crimes"; not so the villainous women in *The Paradine Case* and *To Catch a Thief*. The complex Judy/Madeleine figure of *Vertigo* appears fully culpable in a murder scheme yet can also be seen as the instrument of men (first Elster, then Scottie) throughout the film; the title character of *Marnie* is a full-fledged crook, albeit one capable of redemption.

The notion of a therapeutic theme comes primarily from Robin Wood, who suggests that certain Hitchcock characters are "cured of some weakness or obsession by indulging it and living through the consequences."[9] Wood cites *Suspicion* as a major instance of this motif, and one can find it in many other films; *Vertigo* is especially interesting here, since its "therapy" is physically as well as psychologically on display in the last scene, where Scottie's action (climbing the stairs with Judy in tow) amounts to a self-administered dose of the "flooding therapy" practiced by neobehaviorist clinicians.

Finally, the theme of a knowledge–danger equation has received too little attention from Hitchcock critics, although it runs loudly and clearly through a great deal of his work. The title *The Man Who Knew Too Much* adds little to spectator understanding of either version of that story, but the fact that Hitchcock used it twice over, some 20 years apart – and alludes to it elsewhere, most notably in *Rear Window* – suggests its importance for him. His films often contain individuals who face danger or adventure only after learning some piece of information, be it a secret (*Shadow of a Doubt*), a clue to a secret (*The Lady Vanishes*), the mere fact that a secret exists (*The 39 Steps*), a secret that only appears to exist (*Vertigo*), or whatever "MacGuffin" the scenario has up its sleeve. (Hitchcock used the term "MacGuffin" to mean a plot element that didn't interest him specifically but served to generate and propel the action of a film.)

Although long-studied themes such as those discussed so far are important to Hitchcock's work, others – long neglected by Hitchcock critics – are manifested no less consistently in his films. A crucial one is the deep-seated resonance between "real life" and the world of theater – or rather, the borderline between truth and illusion that theater often represents.

To some degree, of course, we all shape our behavior (in public, at least) in accordance with our awareness of people around us; this is part of what it means to be integrated with a society and a culture. In films, this dimension of behavior often goes unexplored, since filmmakers and audiences take it for granted, overlook it, or simply ignore it. Some filmmakers have probed it, however, paying special attention to the capacity of human beings to reinvent their personalities in accordance with changing circumstances. Theater is often a metaphor in such films, but the theatrical world need not be explicitly present. Although theatrical ambience has a strong presence in *Murder!* and *Stage Fright*, it is absent in *I Confess* and *Rear Window*, which show an equally strong fascination with role playing and behavioral artifice.

Even when no obviously theatrical (or cinematic) activity appears within a Hitchcock film, his characters are forever playing roles, for each other and for themselves. The wide range of these roles is apparent from even a few examples – the policeman's hypocritical pose in *Blackmail*, the professor's feigned respectability in *The 39 Steps*, the heroine's ostensibly loving marriage in *Notorious*, the Uncle Charlie sham in *Shadow of a Doubt*, the false Arab in *The Man Who Knew Too Much* (1956), the Madeleine/Judy masquerade in *Vertigo*, and of course, Norman Bates's mind-bending "portrayal" of his mother in *Psycho*.

Hitchcock's characters "act" for more than one audience, moreover. They perform for one another's benefit – whether the motive is to seduce, deceive, cheat, or simply communicate – in the various schemes that generate and sustain their narratives. They perform for their own gratification or protection, à la Norman Bates. They perform for us as we watch their movies. And they perform for Hitchcock himself, whose camera observes and records their activities. Hitchcock, furthermore, can be considered a performer in his own right – explicitly in his cameo appearances; and implicitly as he manipulates the figures in his films, who act *for* him on-screen.

Every narrative filmmaker sets characters in motion, of course, and thenceforth controls (actively or passively) their every move. Hitchcock stands out by virtue of the ingenuity and thoroughness with which he accomplishes this – through his inventiveness in devising narratives and characterizations and through the meticulousness of his preproduction, shooting, and editing strategies. As the dominating force of a filmic universe that incorporates an unusually large share of violent and immoral actions, however, the "master of suspense" is implicated in an unusually large share of unpleasant activity – from, say, the (passive) voyeurism of *Rear Window* to the (active) savagery of *Frenzy*.

This doesn't mean Hitchcock is a perpetrator of perverse or antisocial acts, to be sure; he merely contemplates and re-creates them, and sometimes even this seems to make him uncomfortable – one thinks of Jefferies, that eager voyeur, averting his eyes (albeit not very often) during *Rear Window*. Given the large quantity of evil deeds that appear in Hitchcock films, one might think he reveled in such things, and one might expect his work to be infused with an atmosphere of perverse pleasure. Perhaps because of his early life in bourgeois Catholic circumstances, however, the mood is often closer to brooding guilt, which generates such powerful momentum that (along with other factors involved in his filmmaking) it actually prevents many stories from achieving the customary closure of a happy, or at least resolved, ending: Think of the moral tensions in the last scene of *Blackmail*, the mental anguish that lingers beyond the last scene of *The Wrong Man*, the ambiguous last image of *Vertigo*. The characters themselves seem to feel this troubled atmosphere, which might be called an "overflow of guilt" from the director's restless and uneasy mind – and from the restless and uneasy culture that shaped, influenced, and enclosed this mind.

What distinguishes Hitchcock's relationship with his characters is not only the importance he attaches to having them under his highly judgmental gaze, but also his willingness to allow them an intuitive knowledge that some kind of presence is overseeing their words and deeds. In a number of his films, a moment arises when a character's behavior seems to reflect awareness (perhaps prompted by a strategically placed on-screen element) of the filmmaker's gaze; of its morbid, yet clinically detached fascination; and of the manipulations in which the filmmaker is engaged.

In some cases, an on-screen character may embody the Hitchcockian gaze, as young Charlie does in *Shadow of a Doubt* when she looks at Uncle Charlie on the stairs of the family house, and the latter is frozen in his tracks (at the exhilarating moment when, in the logic of the narrative, he might believe his criminal secrets will be safe forever) by an overwhelming sensation of something as close to guilt, or the fear growing out of guilt, as he is capable of feeling.

In other cases, a character may respond directly to Hitchcock's unseen yet evident manipulation of the cinematic world. At a key moment in *Vertigo*, for instance, a stable visited earlier in the narrative by Scottie and Judy/Madeleine swings into view behind them as they exchange a particularly significant kiss. Scottie momentarily stops kissing and takes on a perplexed expression, as if he were aware of the cinematic event taking place behind him even though he isn't looking at it. In one sense, of course, he needn't look to be aware of it, since it represents (symbolically and atmospherically) memories called up in his own troubled mind by this close encounter with the re-created woman of his dreams. Yet the stable appears *prior* to his perplexed look, not simultaneously with it, allowing it to be read as a purely cinematic event generated not by Scottie's mind but by Hitchcock's, and taking Scottie (as well as the spectator) by surprise. What's audacious here is less the event itself – although it is a stunning *coup de cinéma* – than the boldness of allowing Scottie a response that visibly acknowledges the filmmaker's active control over the moment, and hence stretches the concept of classical Hollywood narrative to (and probably beyond) its breaking point.

Perhaps because of such awareness of directorial control, the "performances" given by characters within Hitchcock films are often not of the healthy and extroverted kind that lead to creativity and emotional liberation. On the contrary, they tend toward such negative goals as deceit and the manipulation of helpless or ignorant others. Frequently they maintain a morbidly inclined appearance of "being on best behavior" that underlines the powerful superego drive pervading Hitchcock's oeuvre.

Hitchcock's presence in his films is motivated not only by his wish to observe and control – and, particularly, to control *by* observing – but also by a constant quest for *closeness* to his characters, which finds its most potent expression in two practices. One is his celebrated use of point-of-view shots – often praised for their power to generate physical and psychological identification between spectator and character, but equally effective in uniting a character's consciousness and perspective with that of the director himself. The other is Hitchcock's habit of injecting himself – more insistently than other filmmakers, and using methods unlike those of other filmmakers – into the world of his films. He does this not by *becoming* a character, in the manner of a Charles Chaplin, Orson Welles, or Woody Allen, but in two other ways: through his famous cameo appearances, which allow him to enter the action directly, costumed yet unmistakably himself, and through his use of characters and objects that serve as surrogates for his own presence.

Hitchcock's walk-on appearances are traditionally seen as a sort of trademark or public-relations gimmick, as an ongoing cinematic joke with no particular meaning or importance, or as a series of minor directorial grace notes tacked gratuitously onto the films in which they appear. On occasion, however, they have been taken seriously. Ryall, discussing "qualities of self-consciousness ... at odds with the anonymity associated with the tradition of classical film making," calls them "that most familiar mark of Hitchcock's personalisation of his films."[10] More elaborately, Ronald Christ relates the director's "signature appearances" to the *parabasis* convention in Greek Old Comedy, whereby the Chorus speaks directly to the audience (in a

11

moment with "nondramatic" and "illusion-breaking" functions) on behalf of the author.[11]

While these notions are useful, reasoning on the subject can be carried further. Hitchcock's cameos are self-publicizing jokes and ironic punctuation marks, no question about it. They also have perkily nondramatic and illusion-breaking qualities. Yet our willingness to point and chuckle at them needn't stop us from seeing them as something more resonant: manifestations of Hitchcock's deep-seated wish not only to speak *through,* but to become physically integrated *with,* his films.

Blackmail, his first sound picture, provides an example. Hitchcock plays his cameo as a passenger on a bus. A little boy in an adjacent seat annoys him; he complains to the child's parents; the boy turns toward him with an aggressive stare, which Hitchcock returns with a confounded, helpless, and quite comical look. Hitchcock is obviously being menaced by the child – a situation that meshes with the story of the film, which involves the killing of an artist by a woman who is smaller and probably younger than he. (In another echo, just moments after the Hitchcock cameo, the two main characters are almost kept out of a restaurant by a young male doorkeeper.) Clearly the cameo (which has complexities beyond those cited here) functions as a microcomedy that anticipates, and comments on, situations that will figure in the main body of the film. Just as clearly, the cameo could have been realized with a conventional actor, but takes on special resonance (and humor!) by incorporating the filmmaker's own recognizable presence, crammed with good-natured ostentation into an already crowded mise-en-scène.

Three observations can be made concerning this and other cameos. First, Hitchcock enters his movies not only to wink and wave at his audience, but to comment on the action in some small, sly way that accords with the manipulative, often sardonic attitude that characterizes much of his work in general. Second, his presence indicates a wish to approach and "keep an eye on" his characters. Third, the cameos signal to his audience (which normally receives the message on a subliminal level) that he is the presiding spirit of his films. Each movie posits a particular relationship between its characters, on one hand, and fate – or destiny, luck, the way of the world – on the other. In every case, it is Hitchcock who has determined what kind of relationship this will be and how it will work itself out through narrative mechanisms. His on-screen presence is a mischievously overt signature that proclaims his control over the narrative and the world that it constructs.

Hitchcock also developed an indirect way of maintaining a dynamic presence in the world of his films: positioning surrogates (human or not) within certain shots and sequences. I don't mean to suggest that a carefully determined series of Hitchcock "stand-ins" must be detected or decoded in film after film; nor do I suggest intentionality or even full consciousness of the surrogacy practice on Hitchcock's part. I do assert that his iconography often includes human (or humanlike) figures and faces that have no necessary function in the mise-en-scène, or which carry a weight out of proportion to the function they do have, and that these can be taken as signifiers of the filmmaker's presiding influence over the narrative.

Returning to *Blackmail*, we find a number of examples. The most obvious is the painting of a laughing jester – one of Hitchcock's most famous early images – that greets the heroine on her arrival in the room where she will soon (to her own horror) kill a man. The painting mutely witnesses this event; later, it hovers in the police station where the killing is being investigated; still later, it punctuates the last scene of the story with its silent, sardonic merriment. This painted image has been variously interpreted, most usefully as Hitchcock's purest exercise in the "Kuleshov effect," whereby a single image may take on different meanings according to the context in which it is seen. Yet it may also be taken as a signifier of Hitchcock's control over the narrative and of the shifting (perhaps ambiguous) nature of his own sardonic feelings about the events of the story.

Other directorial surrogates in *Blackmail* include the mask in the artist's apartment and the impassive British Museum sculpture that presides over a vain flight toward safety by the film's ostensible villain. (These scenes will be considered at length in the next chapter.) Surrogates in other films include the circus audience in *Murder!*, certain figures in the courtroom of *The Paradine Case*, the Statue of Liberty in *Saboteur*, and the Mount Rushmore faces in *North by Northwest*, among many possible examples. At times Hitchcock blends a cameo appearance with an image that would have a surrogacy function if he weren't present, as in *The Lodger* and *Frenzy*, where he appears in crowds gawking at violent events. Images with a surrogacy function may also serve other, perhaps more important functions at the same time. And full-fledged characters can serve as surrogates. In a discussion of *Vertigo*, one commentator says it is "typical of Hitchcock's work" that he "presents a version, or an understanding, of directorial powers through a surrogate within the film," adding however that "he systematically distinguishes himself from that surrogate and what he represents"; specifically, in *Vertigo* "the Novak figure represents the film and Hitchcock" while "the Stewart figure stands in for those viewers whose attachments elsewhere make them incapable of acknowledging the film or its maker."[12] Characters stand for Hitchcock in other films, as well, including *The Paradine Case* and *The Trouble with Harry.*

Hitchcock's cameos and surrogates thus connect his function as film creator with the content of the films themselves. This gives him a unique position vis-à-vis his narratives, shifting his voice into a subtle, yet tenacious first-person stance, like that of a novelist who abjures an omniscient, godlike perspective by injecting an occasional "I" into an otherwise "objective" flow of prose. In assuming this position, especially through cameos, Hitchcock takes on the nature of an immanent Old Testament deity willing to walk occasionally in the garden with those into whom he has breathed life. By the same means, he displaces his own superego battles into the world of his films — making it clear that the eyes of the father (or the "fathers and the law," in the psychoanalytic language of Jacques Lacan) are always on his characters, and often embodying those eyes (compulsively, yet courageously) in his own on-screen persona.

Another issue raised by Hitchcock's cameos is his relationship — as an on-screen presence — to the fully developed characters in his films. Is he with or against them? like or unlike them? connected or unconnected to them? The answer can generally be found in the mood of benign detachment that typifies his appearances: He pictures himself as a comically inflected, almost painfully ordinary character in most cases, dropping into but barely participating in the world of the story and never suggesting an air of superiority to the characters around him. Still, we may see the very tangentiality of his stance as further evidence that his incursions have another, unstated function: that of keeping his narrative symbolically under control, and of metaphorically spying on his characters — asserting his closeness to them, and his power over their world, from the nearest possible vantage point.

Again, none of this is meant to suggest that Hitchcock consciously thought of a cameo appearance as a full-fledged entry into the world of a film. What he did seek and find, on an intuitive level, was a sense of participation in that world, and an intimacy with it that few other directors have shown any evidence of wanting or needing. In so doing, he also achieved a symbolic oneness with the action — with situations and characters that sprang from his imagination but seemed beyond his control once captured "out there" on celluloid.

This raises a fascinating psychological paradox. One reason for making films (and other artworks) is precisely to seek dominion over thoughts, feelings, and memories that are disturbing, painful, frightening, or somehow forbidden, by "projecting" them into the outside world, where they can be perceived as external and therefore manageable or avoidable. It is tempting to speculate, however, that exorcizing his demons made Hitchcock *lonely*, in a sense, and that he wanted to keep their company even as he cast them out – the mark, perhaps, of a particularly (and audaciously) retentive personality who needed to develop the skills and sensibilities of a first-rate artist in order to pull off a rejection/internalization maneuver of astonishing complexity. Hence, his willingness to make films that manifested his deepest fears of annihilation, violation, and other chaotic eruptions; hence also, his eagerness to venture *into* the land of re-created nightmares, in person (via his cameos) or through surrogate figures and fixtures. Hitchcock has been praised for his ability to "get into the minds" of his characters, and to get *us* there at the same time – by brilliant use of identification techniques and point-of-view manipulations, and (occasionally) through what might be called physical incursions by the camera. This is all part of his urge to draw superhumanly close – physically, psychologically, spiritually – to the world of his own mind, through its objectification in the world of film.

From such considerations, it is clear that Hitchcock's movies are powerfully shaped by his personality, sometimes in obvious ways and sometimes in ways that only the most thorough analysis (biographical as well as theoretical) could fully discover. Yet it may seem that one of the most celebrated aspects of Hitchcock's personality has been deemphasized in my arguments so far: its capacity for jesting, mischievous behavior that delights in debunking, deriding, and deconstructing its own proudly puckish fictions. Are his films really angst-ridden exercises in spontaneous self-expression, or rather – more realistically, not to mention more entertainingly – are they elaborate jokes by a master manipulator who likes to fill the air with flamboyant flourishes before pulling yet another dead rabbit from yet another cinematic hat?

Anybody who has seen Hitchcock on television, tweaking everyone from the network and the sponsor to the audience and himself, knows the pleasure he took in presenting himself not as an artiste but as an arranger, choreographer, and stage manager of fictions as crafty as they are convincing, as facetious as they are factitious. This image no more defines Hitchcock, however, than does that of the tormented creator working out inner anguish on the screen. If my emphasis leans toward the serious and at times anguished side of his sensibility, it's because the other side – the crafty, prestidigitating side that considered no less a shockeroo than *Psycho* to be an outright and obvious joke – is as plain to see as the corpulent physique that was his most famous trademark. Hitchcock the jester will be encountered less often than Hitchcock the brooder in these pages, but his presence should never be forgotten, because it informs Hitchcock's work in deep and multifarious ways.

Some of Hitchcock's most respected films, of course, manifest more than one facet of his personality at the same time. One such is *Frenzy*, which pungently illustrates the link between his artistry and his psychology. This production brought him back to England after years of professional absence and was widely admired at the time of its release in 1972, although some critics have faulted important aspects of it, from the brutality of its pivotal rape/murder scene to the ostentatious red herrings in its plot. In any case, the picture shows a clear obsession with food, a preoccupation that also dogged Hitchcock in his personal life. *Frenzy* is no easy case of a hungry man packing his movie full of eats, though. Properly examined, it emerges as a complex work charged with oral anxieties and a revealing tendency to couple food imagery with those favorite Hitchcock concerns: sex, violence, and death. (The same linkage can be traced through films of very different periods, finding special strength in *Blackmail, Suspicion, Notorious, Rope,* and *Psycho,* among others.) The film is simultaneously a hugely morbid joke, moreover, complete with wry visual puns linking consumption of food with other forms of orality and voracity, not to mention such a ghoulish trope as finger bones that crack and snap like breadsticks. *Frenzy* is among the works that present Hitchcock's personality at its most gleeful *and* its most sinister – pulling off one macabre jest after another, yet revealing an undercurrent of convulsive gloom just beneath the queasily entertaining surface.

However one chooses to view the manifest content of such a film – whether one faults it as misogynistic, celebrates it for technical ingenuity, or takes some other position – one may find, on a less obvious level, evidence of a broad moral vision that runs through Hitchcock's work. His view of the world as a locus of substantial moral complexity has been studied from multiple perspectives by various critics – some emphasizing a religious ethos, centering on the Catholicism that Hitchcock grew up with but eventually set aside; some stressing ethical concerns from a secular perspective; and some taking a psychological slant, steering us again in the direction of personality study by seeing Hitchcock's morality as an extension of his inner life, which (as Donald Spoto's biography attests) was itself as rich, strange, and tangled as anything in his movies.

While these approaches have yielded valid insights, there is a dimension of Hitchcock's worldview that deserves more emphasis: the ultimate importance in his cosmos not of moral struggle and resolution, but of physical confrontation. Hitchcock is indeed a moralist. Once the ethical and psychological battles of his films have been waged, however, final dispositions usually rest in violence and death.

Western culture today is habituated to and conditioned by art that (especially in its "higher" forms) often partakes of an abstract quality, foregrounding matters of construction and form even in areas where content and meaning would once have received virtually all attention. It is characteristic for sophisticated members of this culture to look through the physical components of complex films, instinctively seeking the psychological, ethical, and sometimes spiritual elements that comprise their "deeper" meanings. This is well and good, except that readings also need to go in the opposite direction – toward physical events, focusing on issues more fundamental than, say, the ordering function of colors and the symbolic value of animals, both of which have played a (deserved) part in Hitchcock criticism. Even close analyses of Hitchcock films tend to race past the *visceral* impact of *physical* events that pass across the screen; and of all these physical events, none has such surpassing importance as death, the final arbiter of most disputes, conflicts, and moral/philosophical problems that the movies pose.

Nor is this importance a straightforward matter of the need for narrative closure. It is easy for a film, even a Hitchcock film, to resolve issues symbolically or metaphorically; moviegoers are familiar with this and are generally satisfied with it when it's competently handled. Hitchcock's penchant for physical confrontations of all sorts, including (and especially) fatal ones, reflects his view that symbols and metaphors are often used to evade the ultimate, violent truths of human experience. The filmic world for Hitchcock is only *secondarily* a place of coded colors, symbolic animals, and other elements with "abstract" meanings – not to mention the jokes and MacGuffins that pepper his work. That world is *primarily* a place where moral, psychological, and metaphorically construed struggles are preludes to, or uneasy substitutes for, the real and profoundly physical conflict that ultimately determines every final resolution of every meaningful event. No moral victory could suffice to vanquish the Nazi in *Lifeboat*, who represents what must be the most dauntingly corporeal form of institutionalized evil to stalk the twentieth century; it is necessary that the narrative's crowd of "good guys" tear him to pieces. This action carries with it a host of moral questions that have preoccupied commentators on the film, but the murder of Willy does not grow out of these moral issues – rather, *they* are by-products of the murderous event, which has its own inescapable life. One can imagine a Hitchcock film without moral resonance, and in some early, minor works he has given us just that. One cannot imagine a Hitchcock film, however, that isn't rooted in the ineluctable physicality of the material world that holds and surrounds his characters.

Not surprisingly, given the conflicts and contradictions that Hitchcock sees as inherent in human nature, the obverse of physical confrontation also plays a key role in his work: a preoccupation with inaction, often carried to the point of paralysis. A striking example occurs at the beginning of *Shadow of a Doubt,* when we see Uncle Charlie lying on his bed, as immobile as a vampire waiting for sunset to free him from his coffin; soon afterward we see young Charlie in a similar position, her immobility rhyming ominously with Uncle Charlie's, although generated by somewhat different forces. Another example occurs in *The Birds,* when Melanie becomes almost catatonic as a result of the traumas she has undergone. In *Spellbound,* a brutalizing past event has frozen John Ballantine not physically but in his psychological trajectory. Hitchcock's richest and most elaborate voyage into the essence of paralysis may be that of *Vertigo,* where (as Robin Wood was perhaps first to observe) the male protagonist is literally suspended during the first scene, and remains in a state of metaphorical suspension (since the movie never shows him escaping from this position) for the rest of the narrative. That is, he is seen to be "suspended" in his work and personal relationships, and he responds to further trauma (in the hospital scene after Madeleine's apparent death) by becoming physically as well as emotionally immobile. Suspension equals paralysis – a suggestive formula that gains in resonance when one considers how hard Hitchcock worked to captivate and transfix his audience by mastering a narrative syndrome known (all too appropriately?) as suspense.

After so much discussion of sinister and somber elements in Hitchcock's work, and due ackowledgment of the jokiness that resides there too, it is important to stress that very different elements can also be found. In particular, love plays an essential part in his films, although not surprisingly it is often explored in counterpoint to more forbidding and threatening experiences. Lesley Brill notes the importance of moments when the heroine (or someone else, occasionally) comes to believe in the hero, as when Lisa begins to share Jefferies's theories and suspicions in *Rear Window*.[13] This not only indicates a frequent Hitchcockian narrative gambit; it sums up a crucial dialectic in his work – between love and faith on the hero's side, doubt and suspicion on the other side, which includes yet-to-be-enlightened heroines, the police, and others representing obstacles to the hero's progress. Such others may be characters, but they may also be metaphorical presences signifying a lack of emotional resilience, which represents for Hitchcock a major stumbling block to truth and sanity. The implacable Mount Rushmore in *North by Northwest* and the rigidly crafted sculpture-face in *Blackmail* are examples – and complex ones, since they are also avatars of Hitchcock's own (implacable) presence and (rigid) control over the film.

Further complicating the situation is the fact that Hitchcock's love–faith/doubt–suspicion dialectic cannot in most cases be reduced to a straightforward conflict between good and evil. It may be seen with equal accuracy as a clash between two forces that have generally positive connotations: love and logic. The police are rarely evil in Hitchcock, but by the same token, their logic and order are rarely very effectual. (Cops tend to be "dull and unimaginative," as the blind man in *Saboteur* says.) By contrast, heroes and heroines tend to have love on their side, often manifested through (among other qualities) a sense of intuition that carries much emotional weight even though it is not connected with logical thought. This intuition may be correct in its conclusions, as with the blind man in *Saboteur,* who helps the hero; with Alicia in *Spellbound,* who learns to put her trust in "instinct and passion" and to "disregard reason";[14] and with Babs Milligan in *Frenzy,* who stays faithful to an accused murderer. Intuition can also be ironically mistaken, as with Lina in *Suspicion,* much of which is structured as a series of (seeming) affirmations and (apparent) reversals of what her instincts tell her. Or it may be tragically mistaken, as with Alice's decision to trust Crewe in *Blackmail* and young Charlie's near worship of her namesake in *Shadow of a Doubt*. A character may change or abandon intuitive notions during the course of a film, but is likely to attach great importance to them until the changes or abandonments take definitive shape, at which point the trajectory of the narrative undergoes a decisive change. This change may be of the positive kind seen in *Rear Window*; but it may also be of the sort typified by *Shadow of a Doubt* or *Vertigo,* where *loss* of faith in a seemingly benign individual carries a protagonist to a troubling resolution.

In addition to tracing themes and practices through films from various phases of Hitchcock's career, one can examine the interaction of diverse influences and impulses within individual films. For an example, consider *Rope* (1948), which raises issues connected with virtually all the major Hitchcock films.

During the 1930s, when Hitchcock consolidated his style, stage plays were a major source of movie material. Hitchcock continued to show interest in stage material long afterward, reflecting the influence of that early period and also his personal fascination with "theatrical" behavior. Beginning with *Downhill* in 1927, 14 of his 53 features are based on plays. One is *Rope,* which involved no fewer than four writers: Patrick Hamilton, author of the original play, Hume Cronyn, who wrote the movie adaptation, Arthur Laurents, who wrote the screenplay, and as final authority, Hitchcock himself.

Rope is widely regarded as Hitchcock's most overtly experimental film, primarily because of its unconventional shooting and editing methods. It is filmed in takes approaching 10 minutes in length, the maximum that could be continuously shot. In addition, most reel-to-reel changeovers are disguised by objects positioned in front of the camera. This creates the illusion of continuous filming (and projecting), contributing to the audience's presumed perception of *Rope* as a drama performed, filmed, and viewed/experienced in real time, without the ellipses (generated mainly through editing) that are an essential part of conventional film syntax.

Hitchcock and Hamilton had different interests and priorities. Hamilton was a successful author and dramatist whose works include the novel *Hangover Square,* the source of John Brahm's 1945 melodrama about an insane composer, and the play *Gas Light,* source of two films about a man who attempts to drive his wife mad.

Hamilton clearly had an interest in insanity, particularly of the criminal variety. Hitchcock was also fascinated by both psychology and crime. In the 1940s alone, his pre-*Rope* pictures include at least five dramas with a *Gas Light*–type atmosphere of domestic morbidity: *Rebecca, Suspicion, Shadow of a Doubt, Spellbound,* and *Notorious.*

But comparison of Hitchcock and Hamilton is complicated by the carefully delineated career track that Hitchcock established for himself. He set about becoming and remaining "the master of suspense" for numerous reasons, including a near-compulsive desire for financial security and career stability. Like most labels that are more conducive to mass marketing than to artistic flexibility, however, the "master of suspense" moniker proved as entrapping as it was stabilizing for Hitchcock's career – playing a strong role in his choice of properties, and confusing his audience when he didn't adhere strictly enough to it. At the same time, Hitchcock remained an artistically ambitious filmmaker who wanted to explore serious issues –

social, philosophical, and cinematic – in serious ways for serious moviegoers. Consideration of any Hitchcock film must take into account the tension between this desire and his wish to be known as a maker of rattling-good thrillers for the widest possible range of spectators.

Hitchcock's choice of *Rope* as a property cannot be ascribed to any great popularity of the play itself. Written in 1929, it had come to seem "stagy and dated" in the eyes of most Hollywood observers by the time Hitchcock took it under consideration in the late 1940s.[15] Looking for projects to launch the production company he was in the process of founding, Hitchcock selected three possibilities – *Under Capricorn* and *I Confess* as well as *Rope* – which were already known in Hollywood as "weak properties that the major companies, using their better judgment, had passed over."[16] This negative assessment is borne out by the fact that *Rope* was derived from a 1929 play, *Under Capricorn* from a 1937 novel, and *I Confess* from a turn-of-the-century drama. All three had not only been rejected by the studio system, but had *stayed* rejected despite the passing of years and the changing of fashions.

The year of *Rope*'s release was not an easy one for Hollywood, moreover. Television was beginning to make a strong impact on the low-culture end of American mass communication, while imported European films served up material for more sophisticated spectators. Hollywood still had a grasp on the middle ground between these extremes, but the properties under Hitchcock's eye at this time were hardly middle-of-the-road entertainments – least of all *Rope,* with its "egghead" characters and unsettling blend of the morbid, the intellectual, and the grotesque. To compete with the major studios at this time, Hitchcock might well have considered ideas that would "challenge the studio system" by being "so radical in content that only an independent could produce them."[17] *Rope,* however, seemed simply out of touch.

What attracted Hitchcock to Hamilton's play, despite these drawbacks, was its combination of technical and thematic interest, its link with Hitchcock's artistic personality, and the connection of all these things with the social, political, and ideological climate of the late 1940s. Together, these considerations were enough to offset the fact that stage plays – designed for presentation under noncinematic circumstances – are not the most likely source of material to stimulate a filmmaker's most deeply cinematic impulses. Hitchcock turned to plays not for superficial reasons, but because of the affinity between his artistic sensibility and the aesthetics of theater. As already discussed, he was fascinated by the slippery relationship between reality and illusion – one metaphor for this being the relationship between cinema (filmed "reality") and theater (staged "illusion"). In *Rope* he brings the reality—illusion/cinema—stage relationship into play on two distinct levels: in his manner of filming the play with a technique (long-take/continuous time) that mimics the stage experience to a degree, and in manipulations of reality and illusion within the film itself.

Hitchcock's choice of *Rope* as a property was therefore closely connected with his decision to film it in the unusual long-take fashion. There are several reasons why he chose this technique, including the following, each of which is partially but not completely sufficient:

1. *Rope* is a motion-picture adaptation of a play, and Hitchcock wanted to preserve the continuous, real-time experience of watching a play unfold onstage. This explanation gains credibility from the facts that Hamilton's play also takes place in real time and is *about* the staging of a theater piece. On the other hand, Hitchcock filmed adaptations of many plays during his career, and on only one occasion did he employ strategies anything like those in *Rope* – in *Under Capricorn*, which comes from the same phase of his career.

2. Hitchcock was enthusiastic about technical challenges throughout his working life. If this urge had been his primary motivation, however, he would probably have fulfilled it in *Rope* itself and not gone on to use similar techniques in *Under Capricorn* a year later – especially since *Rope* had not been particularly well received by critics or audiences. Spoto notes that while some contemporary observers commented on the single set of *Rope*, "no one paid much attention to the ten-minute takes."[18]

3. Hitchcock thought long takes would save money by halving the usual ten-to-twelve-week schedule for principle photography – an attractive idea at a time when Hollywood was experiencing higher production expenses, blocked foreign markets, and antitrust activity.[19] The production did not turn out to be as economical as hoped, however, and later productions confirm that economizing had not become his chief objective in selecting and realizing projects.

Most important of all is the fact that Hitchcock found the themes, language, and characters of Hamilton's play compatible with his own ideas, and the long-take technique was integral to his visualization of them. In particular, the dinner party that takes place in Hamilton's play is an excellent example of performance – that favored Hitchcockian metaphor – in the nontheatrical form that obsessed the filmmaker most: In giving the party, Brandon and Phillip are staging a theater piece, of which they are the stars and the invited guests are the audience. Adding to the richness of this conceit is the fact that Brandon and Phillip are themselves an audience observing the behavior of their guests, who thus become unwitting performers of the piece. Showing the party in seemingly continuous time is Hitchcock's ultimate theatrical trope, since it recalls (albeit with a roving camera) the early filmed-theater technique of shooting an unbroken performance in a single take.

Although he found much to preserve and exploit in Hamilton's play, Hitchcock also changed it in many ways, creating a palimpsest in which Hamilton's work remains visible beneath the overlay of meaning that accrues from Hitchcock's additions, subtractions, and alterations. The film thus combines Hamiltonian characteristics (a penchant for melodrama, "foreign" elements, strongly implied homosexuality, poetic dialogue) and Hitchcockian characteristics (a penchant for "everyday" atmosphere, clearly American characters, sexual signifiers suitable to the Production Code and mass-audience appeal, comparatively prosaic dialogue).

Rope may also be examined in terms of film noir, which was flourishing at the time of this film's production and release. On one hand, *Rope*'s story of murder and discovery, and its theme of guilt–innocence confusion, have well-established connections with the noir cycle. On the other, *Rope* lacks the shadowy visuals and shattered narrative line that characterize many noirs. Hitchcock could have rendered it more noirish with a few simple expedients, such as darkening the secondary characters, filming in black-and-white, as he had done with all his previous films, and heightening the use of expressionistic lighting, shadows, and so forth. This would have put *Rope* more in line with a familiar and accepted style of 1940s filmmaking, and would likely have reduced public disapprobation of the film, which (despite Hitchcock's care to prevent this) resulted in calls for banning and censorship in some localities. It is likely that Hitchcock did not emphasize noir elements in *Rope* (or other films) because of a fear that they might distract attention from his own distinctive stylistic practices – which, as already noted, were responsible for his "master of suspense" reputation and hence for his unique presence in the eyes of the public. He was, after all, one of the few directors with a label comparable to, say, "the Lubitsch touch" or the "genius" of Preston Sturges; and he seems to have felt that additional labeling could only dilute his self-propelled legend.

This analysis of *Rope* emphasizes certain elements – notably source material and genre convention – that need not play an equal role in examinations

23

of other films. In subsequent chapters, I have not sought consistency for its own sake, instead letting my particular responses to each film suggest the approach best suited to it. These responses can be encapsulated as follows, offering a brief overview of the chapters to come:

1. *Blackmail* (1929) represents an early eruption of characteristic Hitchcock themes, including the dangerous woman and the transference and assumption of guilt. Here too is a vivid example of the filmmaker's fascination — anticipating that of Jacques Rivette, another of his French admirers — with the (frighteningly!) ambiguous relationship between art and the routine of everyday life, each seen in turn as threateningly subversive of freedom.

2. *Shadow of a Doubt* (1943) is Hitchcock's most aggressive statement on performance as a strategy for survival (the Uncle Charlie pose) and its flip side, psychosexual chaos and paralysis. The middle-class home becomes a theater, the family becomes a self-tormenting and increasingly impotent group of performers, and the supreme artist (Uncle Charlie) reveals himself as an avenging angel of Miltonian ingenuity and singlemindedness.

3. *The Wrong Man* (1956) has prompted obvious comparisons between Hitchcock and Kafka, but too little attention has been paid to the fact that Henry Fonda's character is anything but innocent, any more than Joseph K. was in *The Trial* before him. Of course, he didn't commit the robberies he's accused of, but a torrent of moral failure surges through his psyche. Notice his grotesquely servile behavior (what a performance!) before the authorities, the disintegration of his ostensibly loved family, and the debilitating anguish that afflicts his wife long after the ambiguous "happy ending" to (every)Manny's odyssey. This is in some respects the purest of Hitchcock films, and perhaps the most maddening on thematic and cinematic grounds, as the director lavishes infinite attention on the smallest minutiae of his painstakingly detailed vision.

4. *Vertigo* (1958) outdoes *Rear Window* as a treatise on voyeurism and further illustrates Hitchcock's penchant for tormenting his heroes, confronting James Stewart's character with an evil so overwhelming (in terms of his own psyche as well as psychosocial taboos) that impotence and paralysis cut to the heart of the ostensible plot resolution. This complex melodrama also marks a key step in Hitchcock's adoption of pulp-fiction conventions as expressive devices.

5. *Psycho* (1960) is Hitchcock's nastiest meditation on performance as a way of life, the home as theater and prison, and the predominance of

physicality over psychology and morality in the world of film. Complicating the schema is Hitchcock's deep loathing of the body, unleashed here as never before and touching off a tidal wave of cinema as nausea.

6. *The Birds* (1963) shows chaos inheriting the earth, becoming literally a force of nature and prompting Hitchcock to remarkable fits of obsessive control, not least of which is casting Tippi Hedren in a role that gives (partly unwitting) new meaning to the idea of psychosexual moribundity. The self-aware fabrications of this film – to be topped by those of *Marnie* soon after – call attention to Hitchcock's artifices in a whole new way, crowding their beauties and grotesqueries into a single, surprisingly harsh spotlight. The last great Hitchcock film is also the ultimate Hitchcock film, for better and for worse.

Looking back on these and other Hitchcock films, from *The Pleasure Garden* (1927) to *Family Plot* (1976), a question that keeps arising is why he was drawn so persistently to horrific subjects, and to the subject of horror itself, over the course of an outwardly contented and successful life. Although no complete solution to this mystery rests in the biographical record, one of the most suggestive pieces of anecdotal evidence I have encountered came to me from scholar and archivist Vlada Petrić, who interviewed Hitchcock in 1951. When he was still young enough to be sleeping in a crib, Hitchcock said, he was once badly frightened by a huge, terrifying face that abruptly lunged into view above him; he recognized it as his mother's only after a brief, but severe eruption of fear and panic. This incident (whether wholly true or embellished by memory and fantasy) relates not only to Hitchcock's generalized fears, but to the many "guilty women" who populate his narratives and to the female figures that provide some of his most audacious *visual* coups – ranging in appearance from the hideous skull-face of Mrs. Bates to the shadowy nun who precipitates the last moment of *Vertigo*.

The most reliable information about an artist's work, however, lies more within the oeuvre itself than in biographical details. Hitchcock scattered clues to the interpretation of his work (and life) throughout his films, sometimes with surprising frankness and transparency – and not entirely in his greatest, most imposing pictures. Although his masterpieces must command the most energetic efforts of critics and scholars, a close look at seemingly minor efforts can pay surprising dividends.

There may be no movie, for instance, in which Hitchcock stands more easily and good-naturedly visible than *The Trouble with Harry,* his mildly dark and mildly amusing comedy of 1955. Here the primary Hitchcock surrogate is virtually Hitchcock himself, come to guide us personally through the narrative. This character is known as the Captain, a title that lets us know immediately he's in charge of this excursion. Sure enough, he begins it by taking control of the action (he's the first of many characters to claim responsibility for killing Harry, who's dead before the story starts) and delivering soliloquys toward the camera. He is Hitchcockian in personal terms, too: both English and chubby. He tells of many exciting experiences as a world traveler but finally acknowledges that his voyages were in his imagination – he is a fictioneer, not a buccaneer. He also admits, often and without being asked, to a deep-seated fear of police and their "psychological" methods.

Other characters in the film include a doctor and an artist; there is little doubt that the Captain and Hitchcock sympathize almost entirely with the latter (who clearly has control over his life) rather than the former, whose intellectual abilities don't prevent him from seeming ineffectual and silly – not unlike the local deputy sheriff, who doesn't even have intellectual abilities to lend him an occasional semblance of dignity.

The body of Harry is the real hero of this movie, of course – a whimsical reincarnation of HCE from *Finnegans Wake,* not to mention every corpse from Hitchcock's own corpus. But the Captain is the film's presiding spirit, a mixture of affability, befuddlement, and sly chicanery that Hitchcock seems delighted to offer as a substitute for himself. Like the Captain, he rarely admitted the depth of his thoughts, his passions, or his fictions. Also like the Captain, he made a vivid impression on those who encountered his tales.

Notes

1. Tom Ryall, *Alfred Hitchcock & the British Cinema.* Urbana: University of Illinois Press, 1986.
2. William Stott, *Documentary Expression and Thirties America.* Chicago: University of Chicago Press, 1986, p. 77; Agee quote, p. 76.
3. Ryall, pp. 60–1.
4. Ryall, p. 177. See also Lindsay Anderson, "Alfred Hitchcock," in *Focus on Hitchcock,* ed. Albert J. LaValley. Englewood Cliffs, N.J.: Prentice-Hall, 1972, pp. 48–59.
5. Quoted in Ryall, p. 177.
6. Alfred Hitchcock, "Direction," in *Footnotes to the Film,* ed. Charles Davy, New York: Oxford University Press, 1937, pp. 3–15, cited at 14; reprinted in LaValley, *Focus on Hitchcock,* pp. 32–9, cited at 38.
7. M. M. Bakhtin, *The Dialogic Imagination,* ed. Michael Holquist, trans. Caryl Emerson and Michael Holquist. Austin: University of Texas Press, 1981, p. 426, glossary.

8. Tania Modleski, *The Women Who Knew Too Much: Hitchcock and Feminist Theory.* New York: Methuen, 1988, p. 107.

9. Robin Wood, *Hitchcock's Films Revisited.* New York: Columbia University Press, 1989, p. 71.

10. Ryall, p. 165.

11. Ronald Christ, *"Strangers on a Train:* The Pattern of Encounter," in LaValley, *Focus on Hitchcock,* p. 106.

12. Marian E. Keane, "A Closer Look at Scopophilia: Mulvey, Hitchcock, and *Vertigo,"* in *A Hitchcock Reader,* ed. Marshall Deutelbaum and Leland Poague. Ames: Iowa State University Press, 1986, pp. 231–48, cited at 246.

13. Lesley Brill, *The Hitchcock Romance: Love and Irony in Hitchcock's Films.* Princeton, N.J.: Princeton University Press, 1988, p. 63.

14. Thomas Hyde, "The Moral Universe of Hitchcock's *Spellbound,"* in Deutelbaum and Poague, *A Hitchcock Reader,* p. 156.

15. Leonard J. Leff, *Hitchcock and Selznick: The Rich and Strange Collaboration of Alfred Hitchcock and David O. Selznick in Hollywood.* New York: Weidenfeld & Nicolson, 1987, p. 268.

16. Ibid.

17. Ibid.

18. Donald Spoto, *The Dark Side of Genius: The Life of Alfred Hitchcock.* Boston: Little, Brown, 1983, p. 308.

19. Leff, *Hitchcock and Selznick,* pp. 266–75, gives a convincing account of Hitchcock's wish to counter his growing image as an unpredictable and potentially profligate filmmaker – a budding Orson Welles, one might say.

2

Blackmail

TRACY: . . . he's playing with fire, and we shall all of us burn our fingers. . . .

Hitchcock began his feature-directing career with *The Pleasure Garden* in 1927, a respectable, if not very exciting, debut effort. He followed this with other silent films of varying quality, many of which are still remembered for some visual or narrative idea that prefigures the full-fledged artistry of his later work. *The Lodger* (1927) is generally thought of as the first truly Hitchcockian film, but other movies of the period also contain elements that would figure importantly in his pictures for decades to come – *The Manxman* (1929), for instance, which introduces (as Donald Spoto notes) the image of a threatening bird and also an ancestral portrait that symbolizes family tradition.[1] *Blackmail*, also made in 1929 and inaugurating Hitchcock's sound-film period, has a strong claim to being his first masterpiece.

For modern moviegoers who are most familiar with Hitchcock's full-color, big-star American pictures of the 1950s and 1960s, *Blackmail* must come as a surprise. It's photographed in unspectacular shades of black and white, like all Hitchcock pictures before 1948, and the closest thing to a Hollywood star it offers is Cyril Ritchard in a role that's nasty, brutish, and short. Some of its images and montage devices do have the ring of "pure Hitchcock" as defined by later films. Yet other aspects are unusual by any standard, beginning with the peculiar fact that the first 15 minutes look very much like a silent film.

The excellent reason for this is that *Blackmail* was initiated as a silent production. John Maxwell, the chief executive of British International Pictures – with whom Hitchcock signed a multipicture deal in 1926 – bought

28

the rights to Charles Bennett's hit play *Blackmail* for Hitchcock to direct. Working on the screenplay in late 1928, Hitchcock fashioned an adaptation "even darker than Bennett's original," in Spoto's words,[2] and by February 1929 the cameras were ready to roll. Editing was to start in early April, when Maxwell informed Hitchcock that he had acquired a batch of RCA sound equipment from the United States. Ultimately the film was prepared in two versions: silent for the majority of theaters, but with sound for theaters equipped to handle it. The advent of sound was, of course, exactly the sort of technical challenge that Hitchcock welcomed throughout his career — although he greeted this development with some skepticism at first, concerned that sound would displace "the technique of the pure motion picture."[3]

Even in its talkie version, *Blackmail* begins in a standard silent-movie way, with only a music score and sound effects to be heard; dialogue enters later, after a long and action-packed introduction showing the methods of the London police as they capture a criminal who plays no further part in the story. From there on, *Blackmail* is a sophisticated sound production, showing no evidence of being a first-time effort for either Hitchcock or the British film industry. Indeed, the movie contains at least two uses of sound that are striking — and daring — even by comparison with much later pictures: a scream that links the heroine's traumatized consciousness with the discovery of a corpse, and a monologue in which one nightmarish word ("knife") becomes all the tormented main character can hear.

Hitchcock composed his films with meticulous care, planning every aspect of form, composition, movement, and performance. This makes the practice of close reading especially productive when applied to his work, since it is likely that any given detail was determined by the filmmaker and is not the result of chance or the routine outcome of standardized filming and editing practices. The silent-movie beginning of *Blackmail,* moreover, allows even casual audiences to concentrate fully on matters of montage and mise-en-scène, with no verbal activity to demand attention. So it will be useful to move through this film step by step, examining its details and their implications.

The film begins with one of Hitchcock's audacious abstract shots: the full-screen image of a rapidly spinning disk. This dissolves to the second image, a police vehicle (the disk was one of its wheels, we now realize) on an emergency call. Subsequent shots introduce us to the drivers, and to police officers in the back with radio gear and other paraphernalia. A pan rotates us 180° as the van makes a hairpin turn — indicating the vehicle's flexibility, the movie's high visual energy, and the filmmaker's active presence behind the camera.

The police leave the van through flaps of fabric at the back, surrounded by a cloud of smoke or dust. Like all the images at the beginning of the film, this has a fairly straightforward "documentary" look, implying that we are watching not a constructed dramatic scene but an event taken from (or at least closely resembling) everyday life. Examined in the context of other Hitchcock films, however, it contains a familiar Hitchcockian reference: The flaps resemble a curtain, and the police officers' action resembles the start of a theatrical performance. This effect is likely to be subliminal for the first-time spectator who is not actively hunting for metaphors; yet it is heightened by its position at the opening of the film, when the figures on-screen are indeed commencing the activities of the narrative. Spectators familiar with Hitchcock's earlier and subsequent films may connect this with other "theatrical" touches such as (among countless examples) the baroque costuming that helps give the title character of *The Lodger* his menacing appearance.

Hitchcockian motifs of other kinds soon follow. The police walk through an underpass, moving past children playing some aggressive game; the underpass resembles a tunnel, suggesting confinement yet also movement and progress, while the youngsters help establish a mood of (aggressive) action. The presence of children in Hitchcock almost invariably suggests some kind of actual or incipient chaos — a fact borne out in later films as different as *Spellbound* and *Marnie* — and this is no exception.

Pushing their way past a distraught woman, the cops enter a building where two of them climb a stairway, then walk down a corridor to a featureless and rather forbidding door. Here, still in the opening moments of the film, are icons signaling three more Hitchcock preoccupations: Stairs indicate the possibility of movement to a new plane of action and experience, its nature still unknown. (Lesley Brill has convincingly shown that movements *up-* and *down*stairs have different, and frequently drastic, connotations in Hitchcock movies.) Corridors, like the tunnels already mentioned, present confining conditions while also indicating the need to traverse physical and/or emotional terrain. Doors conceal unknown challenges and dangers, although in some circumstances they represent possibilities for growth and enrichment, as well. The presence of all three motifs at the beginning of *Blackmail* — and in a portion of the movie that stands apart from what will become the main narrative — shows Hitchcock's early fascination with the possibilities of architectural imagery, which he would continue to exploit throughout his career.

Pushing the door open, the police see a man lying in bed, reading a newspaper that hides his face. Pictured in close-up, he looks like a stock villain, with messy hair and a cigarette jutting out of his mouth. Following his gaze, the camera pans across the room, to a mirror reflecting the cops' faces.

This is a superbly Hitchcockian sequence. The newspaper divides the villain from the onlookers in exactly the way that a curtain hides an actor from an audience before a performance. This introduces the concepts of illusion and (false) appearance into the film, since the villain appears more helpless than he really is, and the police are functioning as spectators at a show that he is spontaneously "staging" for them. The pan shot, following the villain's gaze, stresses the all-important function of looking and seeing in Hitchcock's work. Meanwhile, the view of the police, darkly framed in the mirror, makes them look as sneaky, shifty, and sinister as the man they've come to apprehend, especially since their bodies are crossed by blunt shadows from the window's venetian blinds.

Still hidden by his newspaper "curtain," the villain moves his gaze to a gun on a nearby table; the police stare implacably at him; and in another remarkable image, we see the gunman's hand moving slowly toward the weapon, his face and arm shadowed on the wall in a distorted shape that recalls the vampire of F. W. Murnau's *Nosferatu*. (Vampire references will have later resonance in Hitchcock's career, notably in *Shadow of a Doubt*.) As he grabs for the gun, his hand becomes visible alongside the newspaper. The police leap in and struggle with him, their overcoats hiding the action from us (another curtain effect) until they seize the gun and move it briefly into our view. After a bit of conversation, the police bring the villain his clothes — asserting their new control over his "performance" by determining the costume he will wear — and he dresses, punctuating his "act" with a broad grin when the stagelike space of his room is invaded by a rock hurled through the window by a hostile neighbor outside. The police escort him through the "curtain" at the back of their van, ending this portion of the drama.

The next portion brings us to New Scotland Yard, where the police take their prisoner down a long corridor that recedes into the depths of the frame. As he is interrogated, the length of the procedure is measured by the accumulation of cigarette butts in an ashtray, a device that not only shows Hitchcock's flair for economy at this early stage of his career, but provides an intimate, even grubby detail that contrasts effectively with the next sequence: the singling out of the arrested man in an "identification parade" (another kind of theater or spectacle) before he is formally charged. Like the sequences that precede it, this section of the film is shot and edited in a documentary (or docudrama) style that establishes an atmosphere of harsh realism; later this atmosphere will enhance the *verismo* credibility of the purely dramatic scenes that are the film's main interest. The style also reflects Hitchcock's morbid fascination with police procedure, of course, every detail of which seems endlessly interesting to him.

Bit by bit, in a maneuver that Hitchcock will repeat in such later films as *The Paradine Case* and *The Wrong Man,* the prisoner's identity is now stripped from him. He is forced to remove his hat, an important part of his "costume." A frontal view of his face, by which the world commonly knows him, dissolves to a close-up of a fingerprint, a detail of his body that only interests those who oppose him. His hands are manipulated in the fingerprinting routine, demonstrating the continuing control of the police over his actions. Eventually he is flung into a cell – and henceforth, despite his importance up to this point, he is forgotten about for the rest of the narrative.

Only now does the camera track *with* the policemen, as they walk down another corridor away from the experiences they've just been through. And only now does the film acquire dialogue and become a talkie in the full sense of the term, beginning with a policeman's offhand remark: "Well, we finished earlier tonight than I expected!"

This line is helpful to an understanding of *Blackmail.* Hitchcock's purpose is to juxtapose highly dramatic events and emotional crises, on one hand, with ordinary routines of everyday living, on the other. Hence, the male protagonist, a police officer named Frank, is seen taking flamboyant events in stride. Soon after the docudrama section of the film is over, he and his colleagues are found in the lavatory – always an important and revealing location in Hitchcock's work – washing their hands after (and of) the physical and moral toil of a day's work. A particularly important image shows a policeman dangling a pair of handcuffs (Hitchcock's favorite symbol for bondage and attachment) conspicuously in front of the camera. Right behind him, two other cops point their backsides (another important symbol for the filmmaker) directly at us.

It is worth pausing here to consider Hitchcock's view of the police. Although he never lost an opportunity for remarking on his distaste for them, he told François Truffaut something more nuanced: "I'm not *against* the police; I'm just afraid of them."[4] In some films, they are seen as genuine (and perhaps indispensable) guardians of order, staving off the chaos that

Hitchcock feared far more than he feared cops. And occasionally they are extremely useful; one thinks of Inspector Hubbard in *Dial "M" for Murder*, whose ostentatiously combed mustache indicates dependability as well as dullness.

The police have a dangerous aspect in *Blackmail*, since they chase to his death a character (Tracy) who is, although sleazy, innocent of the crime he's accused of by the law. They would have no interest in him, however – even a mistaken interest – if Alice White, the film's heroine, had not killed someone. Nor would the police cause Tracy's death if Frank, the film's hero, weren't determined to pin his girlfriend's action on a man who had nothing (directly) to do with it. As seen by Hitchcock's camera, the police in *Blackmail* aren't scary figures. Rather, they're stolid and rather dull professionals (anticipating the *Dial "M"* inspector) who regard their occasionally exciting activities, such as the arrest that opens the movie, as all in a day's work. Hitchcock emphasizes this attitude with his carefully planned display of cops in the men's room, washing up and chattering about nothing at all.

Once it acquires its sound track, *Blackmail* grows more intense. Yet it is often less richly detailed in its talkie phase than in its early, silent scenes – perhaps because Hitchcock did sometimes fall prey to the "photographs of people talking" syndrome despite his own warnings about it, and perhaps because his personal interests led him to lavish his most careful attention on the police and New Scotland Yard sequences. *Blackmail* anticipates many a Hitchcock film (particularly *The Wrong Man*) in its fascination with the pursuit of someone perceived as a wrongdoer. This fascination tends to draw out the best and worst in Hitchcock – eliciting some of his deepest feelings, yet sometimes dampening story and character development as he lingers, almost lovingly, on small details.

Since the opening scenes of *Blackmail* focus on such details, it should be stressed that Hitchcock had at least two motivations for beginning the film as he did. One was his interest in documentary expression, as discussed in the preceding chapter and borne out in other silent (e.g., *The Lodger*) and sound (e.g., *Rich and Strange*) films. Another was his intention of giving *Blackmail* a circular construction in which elements of the first and last scenes would mirror each other. As originally conceived, the story was to culminate with Alice going through the sort of arrest procedure we saw in the opening scenes; then Frank would be seen cleaning up after her arrest, being asked by a colleague if he's going out with his girlfriend that night, and flatly replying that he's going straight home. It would surely have been moving to see Alice, with whom we sympathize so strongly, enmeshed in a process that we have already witnessed in the impersonal context of a "documentary" about a criminal we hardly know. It is doubtful, on the other hand, that the film would have been *more* resonant than in its existing form.

Still, the opening portion is not as steeped in documentary form as one would gather from many descriptions of it. The early images – of the police van, the men and equipment in it, and so forth – could have been excerpted from a genuine documentary. Yet the sequence as a whole is composed, shot, and cut according to fiction-film practices. Even more so, the moment when the wanted man sees his pursuers in a mirror lacks the spontaneity of camerawork and editing that one would normally associate with documentary filmmaking; it may be the absence of a conventional sound track that leads observers to link this highly constructed, traditionally dramatic scene with the somewhat more documentary-like moments that precede it. In a similar case, absence of dialogue gives the beginning of *Rich and Strange* a tone of authority that any documentary might envy, even though this sequence is quite lavish in its use of stylized images and expressionistic devices. Interestingly, both these films establish an early tone that ultimately proves to be in contrast with the real concerns of the story and characters: *Blackmail* begins like a documentary yet turns into a story of great narrative subtlety and moral ambiguity, just as *Rich and Strange* begins with strongly stylized touches only to become an ironic journey *away* from illusion and *toward* the ineluctable realities of the all-too-real world.

Blackmail establishes itself still more securely as a talkie when Frank meets Alice for a date. She begins it by scolding him, because he made her wait 30 minutes in the police station. Then, in a moment that will have reverberations later, she pauses on her way out of the building as a uniformed cop whispers something – evidently a joke – into her ear, causing her to laugh.

The giggling carries into the next shot as she and Frank appear outside. The two do not seem to feel much emotional closeness; their gazes run parallel to each other, not toward each other, as they stand together for the first time. Nor does he seem to be in on the joke between her and the cop. They don't become any more affectionate as they walk away from the station, passing more policemen who fill the screen with their anonymous, vaguely menacing strength – a typical image for Hitchcock, who uses a similar trope in several films. Yet the presence of the police does not cast a pall over the scene; on the contrary, it causes Alice to remember the joke and giggle again.

34

The next scene finds Alice and Frank no closer emotionally but at least facing each other, caught in a noisy streetcar where they can't converse. Distractions include Hitchcock himself, in his cameo appearance discussed in the previous chapter, confirming his presence in the film by confronting an unpleasant little boy. The child also pulls Frank's hat annoyingly over his eyes.

Alice and Frank arrive at a restaurant, jockey for a table, and participate in two important moments. In the first of these, Alice loses a glove, which Frank locates, prefiguring an important plot twist later on; then Alice, the erstwhile giggler, refuses to laugh at a joke that *he* makes at her expense. They continue to banter, Alice still irritated at Frank's lateness and showing no interest in his suggestion that they see a movie called "Fingerprints." It was directed by "a real criminal," she says; Hitchcock is evidently poking fun at himself and his profession. The title "Fingerprints" also recalls the cut between face and fingerprint in the "documentary" prologue, which established the fingerprint as a signifier of impersonality and diminished identity.

Alice peeks at a note she has received, evidently from a man who wants her company that night, and exchanges meaningful glances with someone who appears to be that very fellow. Frank leaves in a huff over her changing moods, then waits outside, only to see her leave accompanied by the man (Crewe, called "the Artist" in the credits) with whom she flirted a few moments earlier. The scene fades out on Frank's perplexed face, accenting his importance as a character – and as the possessor of a gaze that carries significant weight in the narrative – at a time when he will disappear from the film for a while.

Fade in on Crewe's apartment building, pictured (like some other important locations) frontally and uninvitingly. A suspicious-looking man is skulking about, but – despite the strong indication that he will figure in the story – he vanishes as the couple strolls up. In a two-shot, Crewe entices Alice to enter the building and see his studio. This shot, with Crewe positioned on the more shadowy side of the frame, is interrupted by two quick cutaways: one to the suspicious-looking man, who has not entirely left the narrative, the other to the store owned by Alice's father, which she mentions to Crewe.

These cutaways establish two opposite poles of Alice's experience. The store signifies the safe, dull, orderly world of her family and the haven it has presumably offered her from the world at large; the man personifies the lurking chaos of the city and of spontaneous adult life in general – so dimly and briefly perceived as to remain a wholly anonymous threat, but

35

clearly a threat nonetheless. The symbolism here is not particularly subtle, but the elusive/allusive quality of the skulking-man image carries an emotional charge that heightens the effectiveness of the scene and of the events to come.

Alice agrees to visit Crewe's studio, remarking that "it would take more than a man" to frighten her. She also says, in a forceful instance of Hitchcock taking the tragic view of intuition, that a woman knows "instinctively" when she can trust a man. Their entrance into the building is interrupted by the suspicious-looking man, who has returned and speaks with Crewe out of our view. Crewe returns, calling him "nothing but a sponger" who "pesters" people in the neighborhood; the scene shifts inside as the couple passes through the door. The camera peers up the staircase, as Hitchcock cameras often do, emphasizing the dual nature of stairs – at once an obstacle to be surmounted and a route toward new opportunity – and after a pause, during which Crewe looks at his mail and queries his landlady about a letter, he and Alice go upstairs. The camera follows their every step with an elegant crane shot that further heightens the importance, narratively and metaphorically, of this climb. In many respects it recalls the similar moment in Frank Borzage's *Seventh Heaven,* only in this case the destination is less paradisiacal, and Hitchcock's care in rendering the situation seems geared to irony (of a dark, almost grim variety) as well as suspense.

We enter the studio before the characters do, confronting an ominous-looking mask that hangs next to the door; it invokes a primitive mood and suggests the particularly keen interest of Hitchcock (whose face and gaze we must be reminded of) in the events to come. Immediately on arriving, Crewe fiddles conspicuously with the (vaguely theatrical) curtains of his bed. In a quintessential Hitchcock shot that echoes Alice's earlier walk with Frank, she notices a policeman on the sidewalk below – nearby and fully visible through the window, yet oblivious to whatever might be enacted outside his line of vision.

Inside the room she sees a large portrait of a jester that seems to be pointing and laughing at her. The camera pulls suddenly back from it, then cuts to Alice, who giggles at her own nervousness. Leaving the portrait, she walks around the room, whistling and toying with the piano; then she asks Crewe about his palette and canvas. He banters with her, his jacket held back and his hips thrust close to hers, a gesture that reinforces her question's implication of childlike curiosity about Crewe's male secrets. Then he helps her draw a picture that turns into a sketch of a nude woman. Revealing her ambivalence to the situation, Alice tells him he's "awful" but promptly signs the sketch with her own name (Fig. 1).

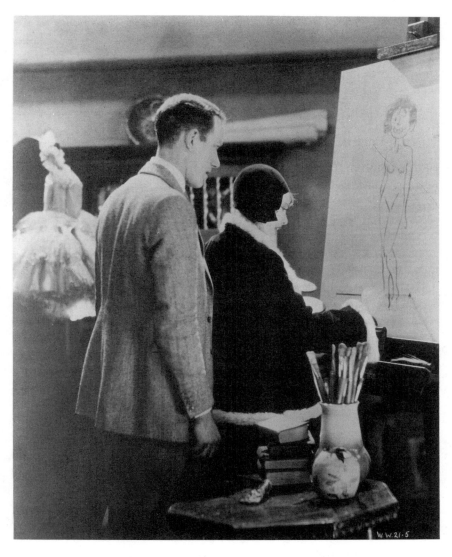

Figure 1. Repressed wishes in the artist's studio: Crewe (Cyril Ritchard) coaches Alice (Anny Ondra) in *Blackmail*. (Museum of Modern Art/Film Stills Archive)

This scene's richness grows not only from the strength of its performances and the nuanced quality of Hitchcock's mise-en-scène and camerawork, but also from its artful use of two key Hitchcockian motifs: that of performance and theatricality, and that of Hitchcock's own presence as presiding influence over the narrative.

The latter motif manifests itself in the mask next to the studio door and in the painted jester. These images, which dominate the film when they first appear, complement each other.

1. The mask, an element of the frame and mise-en-scène, performs a *metaphorical* function by suggesting the primitive nature of Crewe's intentions, which are connected less with "art," despite his label of "Artist," than with aggressive sexuality. It also invokes the presence of the filmmaker as an impassively observing figure who will not impose a moral order or a positive resolution on events that, having been set in motion, are to be propelled by (Crewe's) amorality and (Alice's) fear toward a violent and destructive outcome.

2. The portrait, carrying a weight in the montage approaching (momentarily) that of the living characters, performs the *metonymic* function of displacing Alice's feelings away from herself and into the situation she's confronting – thus visually representing her difficulty in resolving a set of conflicting emotions even as they stare her in the face, courtesy of the filmmaker. (The painting will return to the film more than once, serving related, but different functions each time.)

The performance motif makes itself felt the moment we enter the studio and see the mask, an object so visually striking – and so out of keeping with an "ordinary" or "average" apartment – as to suggest stage dressing. The next clear signifier of theatricality is Crewe's handling of his bed curtains, a gesture indicating that the studio (and particularly the bed itself) is a place where he can arrange and control whatever performances he wishes. Meanwhile the policeman goes through his thoroughly rehearsed paces outside the window; this window also serves Alice as a proscenium, and the spectator of *Blackmail* as a screen within the screen.

Alice's performance is the most spontaneous of the three that figure in the scene, as she whistles and parades about the room. Crewe's is far more calculated, especially as he works his body into its suggestive hips-forward pose. He then takes on the function of director (one of many Hitchcock characters who do so) by guiding Alice in her attempt to mimic *his* role as an artist. The result is a crude painting that makes visible the role he wishes (and she perhaps wishes/fears) she might play. Alice reacts to their joint effort with a disapproval as perfunctory as it is ritualized; and as Robin Wood has noted, she signs it with block letters that could signify the *title* of the painting (*Alice White*), and hence the visible eruption of a repressed wish.

The significance of theatrical motifs in Hitchcock is found in their close connection with the theme of illusion as a key consituent of – and, often, a substitute for – the material reality of everyday life. This theme is strongly felt in the *Blackmail* studio scene. Crewe is consciously playing the (for him) highly artificial role of likable, trustworthy man of the arts. Just as consciously, Alice is playing the role of playful, innocent youngster toying with the appearances but not the realities of sexual availability. The difference between these performances is that Alice believes in hers, which is presumably rooted in her upbringing and in what she believes are the expectations that would automatically be shared by herself and any decent man with whom she might allow herself to become involved. (Frank no doubt shares these expectations, for instance, and might not transgress certain limits even if he and Alice did work themselves into a situation like this one.) Crewe, by contrast, knows that his is an utter sham – and might conceivably believe, or at least want to believe, that Alice also knows this.

The dichotomy between illusion and reality evoked by Hitchcockian performance goes deeper, moreover, than the mere fact of socially, culturally, and sexually determined acting of the kind in this scene. Hitchcock finds the physical world a slippery place where the psychological (e.g., in *Marnie*) and the spiritual (e.g., in *The Wrong Man*) can overlap with materiality; a vivid instance is the moment soon to come in *Blackmail* when Alice's flight from Crewe's apartment is haunted by weirdly transparent figures in the street. Hitchcock's world is profoundly physical, but the precise nature of that physicality is not easily known, and misapprehensions abound. Illusion is everywhere, up to and including the illusory "happy ending" that will conclude *Blackmail* after many further encounters with the blurred boundary between the actual and the apparent.

Alice plunges into the next phase of her performance when a ballerina's dress catches her eye; after some bantering indecision, she agrees to wear it so Crewe can sketch her. This signals a continuing flirtatiousness on her part, and a complicity in the potentially romantic situation that she's burrowing into more deeply by the moment. (In this film, as Brill puts it, "no one can be either entirely pure or wholly inexcusable. Virtually all its action takes the shape of collaboration."[5]) As she changes her clothes, Crewe seems nervous and distracted; perhaps he is wrestling with a growing sense of sexual tension, and perhaps he is neurotic, even dangerously so. He could well be both, a combination not rare in Hitchcock's world.

In a striking shot that creates a split-screen effect, using a dressing-room screen as a curtain, Crewe sings at the piano ("Miss Up-to-Date" is the refrain of his song, meant as a directorial coaching device for Alice) while she puts on the outfit.[6] Each character is now "performing" for the other more openly than ever, in a pas de deux of nervous sexuality and coy hesitation. Hitchcock is obviously enjoying their performances, too; he has framed them in the most artful composition of the movie thus far, encouraging his audience to savor the moment along with him (Fig. 2).

Crewe adjusts Alice's costume when she emerges from behind the screen, then grasps her roughly by the head (a gesture that will recur in *North by Northwest* and elsewhere) and kisses her. She pushes him away and retreats behind the screen, hanging her outfit over the top of it. In a shot Hitchcock spoke of proudly, Crewe is seen with a shadow falling on his face, giving him the curly mustachio of an old-fashioned melodrama villain.[7] He pulls the dress out of Alice's reach and plays the piano more feverishly than ever. (Music and restless movement are his two main outlets for sexual energy, just as they are important ways of building suspense in movies.) Then he pulls her from behind the screen, onto the "stage" of the room. We see the policeman pass obliviously below, then the shadows of Alice and Crewe on the wall as he tries to rape her. The camera pans to the bed; they struggle behind the curtains; her hand emerges and gropes for help; the camera tracks in for a closeup as she seizes a knife from a bedside table. There is a cut as the curtains fall still, and Crewe's hand flops out from behind them, motionless.

Critics have disagreed about exactly what is happening to Alice when Crewe attacks her: Is it a full-fledged rape, some kind of neurotic display of affection, or just an overeager embrace? Much of this debate has centered on the nature of the "evidence" available for us in making our judgment; if Hitchcock does intend us to read the event as an attempted rape, that evidence would naturally be slim, since filmmaking and censorship practices of the period (in Britain and elsewhere) did not allow the depiction or even the strong implication of such an act, which would have to be suggested through exactly the sort of imagery Hitchcock uses. It is certainly possible that Hitchcock intended one of the less-drastic readings mentioned above; but even if this is the case, there is no reason why the confused, eventually terrified Alice might not *consider* it an all-out sexual assault and fight it with any means at her disposal. As to the related question of whether Alice

Figure 2. Miss Up-to-Date: Nervous sexuality and a split screen as Crewe (Cyril Ritchard) and Alice (Anny Ondra) perform for each other in *Blackmail*. (Museum of Modern Art/Film Stills Archive)

"asked for" Crewe's attentions by accepting his invitation, entering his boudoir, putting on a skimpy dress, and so forth, there is no more reason to dignify this blame-the-victim hypothesis in movies than in life. It is Crewe himself who becomes the ultimate victim, of course, by getting killed; but then, he is the one who "asked for it."

Alice emerges and replaces the knife on the table, stricken with horror. She becomes aware of her seminudity, like Eve in the Garden of Eden. Retrieving her dress, she uncovers the picture of the jester; its silent laugh recalls both the insolence of the artist and the sardonicism of the filmmaker who set this whole performance in motion. She lashes out at the painting, punching a hole in the canvas – literally attacking the imagery of the scene. Then she dresses and prepares to leave, in a long shot that turns the room into a stage once more. Before departing, she blacks out the signature/title on the nude sketch, not only covering traces of her visit but disavowing any ownership of what has taken place that night. As she goes down the stairs – which we viewed in a crane shot earlier – they are filmed from above, turning the stairwell into a yawning and threatening pit.

Alice sneaks into the street, and a shadowy figure follows her. So does the camera, in an elegant tracking shot. The atmosphere is charged with her anxiety. Some passersby seem ghostly and transparent, and the arm of a traffic cop (a characteristic Hitchcock control figure) reminds her of Crewe's dead arm protruding from behind the bed curtain. Advertising signs menace her: A theater announces a "new comedy," an illuminated sign bristles with hellish flames, a gin advertisement ("White for Purity") shows a moving cocktail shaker that becomes a stabbing knife in her dazed imagination. As night becomes morning, she is startled by a homeless man, whose outstretched arm echoes her recurring vision of Crewe's arm. Her scream becomes that of Crewe's landlady discovering his corpse. (Cutting on a scream is a gambit Hitchcock will repeat, more self-consciously, in *The 39 Steps*.)

Alice has definitively entered a Hitchcockian realm labeled the "chaos world" by some critics. A characteristic of this realm in certain films, including this one and *Marnie,* is the recurrence of split-screen effects that echo the psychological state (be it distracted, fragmented, or completely shattered) of the afflicted character. At this point a split-screen image shows Crewe's landlady having a difficult time conveying her story to a policeman – a moment that also reflects Hitchcock's idea that the simplest human communications can be nearly impossible to conduct in the stressful times when they are most needed.

After this transitional moment, Frank reenters the picture, helping with the search of Crewe's apartment. He whistles while he pokes around, as Alice did earlier, reinforcing their identity as a couple and anticipating the awful complicity they will soon share. The objects he examines – the painting of the jester, the ballerina dress, the nude sketch – are all artistic extensions of the human body, each with its own place on the continuum between the "real," anchored in fundamental human existence, and the "representative," rooted in illusion and theatricality. He then picks up one of Alice's gloves from the floor, starts to call out his discovery, and stops short when he sees the corpse. The camera rushes toward the corpse with Frank's gaze, then cuts to Frank as he slowly turns away and examines the glove more closely. The jester laughs mirthlessly at him, in close-up, just before he conceals the incriminating glove between his hands. Fade to black.

Alice returns home, mounts (yet another) staircase to her room, and slips into bed just before her mother (whom she barely evaded when entering the house) comes in to wake her. "Anyone'd think you hadn't been asleep all night," says the unconsciously ironic mom. She tells her daughter the latest news of the neighborhood: a nearby murder. Meanwhile, she uncovers a birdcage, from which emerges a stream of chirping and cheeping that continues throughout the scene, adding to the psychological pressure on Alice. This touch shows Hitchcock's immediate mastery of the new sound-movie medium. Birds are one of his favorite symbols for the disorder and chaos of the everyday world, from his early career through such late works as *The Birds* and *Psycho;* here he employs the metaphor with economy and assurance.

Photos on the wall (including one of Frank, in uniform) preside over the room as Alice changes her clothes. Hitchcock's camera is not discreet here; it shows Alice's intimate activity in a montage of close-ups that emphasize her youthfulness and attractiveness. She is performing directly for the camera (and Hitchcock) in this scene, reassuring them (and herself) that she is still a healthy and vibrant young woman despite the trauma she has gone through. She starts the process by putting on makeup at a dressing table, then pulls her new dress from a curtained closet. The camera then frames her entire room frontally, as if it were a stage, before cutting in for close-ups. After changing, Alice walks through her bedroom door and appears at the head of the staircase, carefully preparing her entrance into the next part of the film – a spectacle staged for, as well as by, Hitchcock and his camera.

Downstairs in her father's store, Alice almost telephones the police but loses her courage. Instead, she sits down to breakfast with her family, sparking the film's most brilliant (and, for 1928, astonishing) use of sound. A neighbor gabs endlessly about the local murder. After panning between her and Alice, the camera frames Alice alone in close-up. As she listens, the neighbor's voice turns into gibberish except for the word "knife," which stabs Alice's consciousness each time it's repeated – until she loses her composure while trying to cut her father a piece of bread with a large kitchen knife, and escapes to the store where a customer is waiting. Leonard J. Leff puts the audacity of the "knife" episode in useful perspective when he points out that audiences listened with particular interest for *clarity* of spoken words in early sound films – yet Hitchcock, always willing to follow his own rules, didn't hesitate to muddy his sound track on purpose, creating an aural point-of-view shot that serves the expressiveness of the scene with exemplary precision.[8]

The next sound to pierce Alice's thoughts is the doorbell announcing Frank's arrival. He edges hesitantly into the frame. Telling the family that he's "on" the murder case, he uses a reluctant tone, as if he were ashamed of it. Then he retreats to the phone booth, just missing sight of the "sponger" lurking outside. In the booth, Frank confronts Alice with her lost glove, but before she can respond, the sponger (Tracy) summons them out. He reveals that he has Alice's other glove, and that he plans to blackmail her with it. Hitchcock frames Alice between Tracy and Frank, graphically expressing the helplessness of her position: caught between the law and chaos, and also between two men who feel empowered to control her destiny.

Tracy makes an elaborate production out of lighting a cigar, a phallic interlude that anticipates films as different as *Lifeboat* and *Shadow of a Doubt*. Characters and camera do a good deal of watching and waiting — activities that Hitchcock often turns to poetic effect — as Tracy makes insinuated threats, at which Frank and Alice squirm in discomfort. When he reveals his name and enters Alice's home, the effect is of a character barging into a measured, carefully controlled stage production ("A Merchant-Class London Household," it might be called) from another, far more chaotic play. In a movie full of quintessential Hitchcock moments, this is among the most important, revealing the vulnerability and fundamental weakness of the bourgeois family, never safe from predators and parasites (be they spongers, birds, or mass destroyers of the Uncle Charlie sort) that are always waiting for an opportunity to intrude.

Tracy relaxes in an easy chair, and a cut from him to the jester painting moves us to the police station, where the painting is being held. The landlady, who earlier took a message from Tracy for Crewe, is being questioned. Asked about Tracy's age, she replies that she doesn't know because "he had his hat on," an ironic testament to the power of costuming. A zoom into the policeman's telephone mouthpiece leads to a montage of mugshots, then to a cop being dispatched to arrest Tracy. Hitchcock cuts from the police chief rubbing his hands (the jester painting in the background) to Tracy doing the same, equating the predatory nature of cops and criminals.

By now, Tracy has settled into the White household comfortably enough to whistle "The Best Things in Life Are Free" while wolfing down an extorted breakfast. This causes great chagrin for Alice's mother, whose dislike for Tracy evidences a "good sense" that middle-aged women sometimes have, combined with a sort of bovine silliness, in Hitchcock's films. Her instinct here is certainly more sound than Alice's was when she accepted Crewe's invitation.

Frank gets a call from a colleague: Tracy is being hunted, since he was spotted near the scene of the killing and has a criminal record. Alice's father strains to hear this call, but cannot, since Frank cuts off the sound track of the "performance" by closing the phonebooth door.

Framing and editing take on new expressiveness in the ensuing scene. Frank looks into the other room through the door window, its lower half covered by a curtain that emphasizes the theatricality of the dramatic entrance he is about to make. Entering the room, he is greeted by terrifically anxious looks from both Alice and Tracy, betraying the guilt they feel and the discomfort aroused in them by any new twist in the drama they are playing out. By contrast, Frank is triumphant as he swaggers in and tells Alice to lock the door. His command is accompanied by a pan to the lock and Alice's hand entering the frame to turn it. Gloating openly, Frank reveals his new intention of pinning the killing on Tracy.

Alice is again framed between the two men, as Tracy threatens to tell the police everything *he* knows. She looks worried and guilty, in contrast with Frank as he witheringly reminds Tracy that he's a "jailbird." For a while, all three characters are framed facing the camera rather than each other; their pose emphasizes the formal, set-piece nature of their scene, and also their alienation (no eye contact is possible) from one another.

Frank mentions the "squad van" on its way, and the camera cuts to Tracy as he starts in surprise; then it swings to Alice's anxiety-ridden face as Tracy announces that the van won't be taking *him* away. In a gesture charged with phallic aggression, his finger jabs toward the back of Alice's head as he asserts it will be *his* word against *hers*. Still in the same shot, the camera reframes on Alice and Frank as she implores Frank not to pin the killing on a man who did not commit it; it swings back to Tracy (the starting point of the shot) as she continues to plead. The shot ends, ironically, as Alice enters Tracy's frame while he angrily asks Frank why he won't let Alice speak. As Frank retorts with, "You mind your own business," we return to the three-shot with Alice trapped between the men – one who has tried to blackmail her and one who has been acting toward her like a veritable puppet master.

Tracy is isolated in close-up as he suggests, desperately, that they all drop the matter and go their separate ways. The camera swings past Alice (ignored while the men work out their aggressions) to Frank, also in isolation except for a packet of cash that Tracy extends into the right-hand side of the frame, to be withdrawn – the camera swinging back with it – as Frank disdainfully takes out a cigarette. It pans to Frank and Alice together as Frank lights his cigarette. Entering the shot, Tracy says they're all "playing with fire" and will get burned. Again there's no eye contact as Tracy pleads with Frank

45

– addressing him through Alice, in the third person – and then reiterates that it will be his word against Alice's.

The doorbell rings, and the camera swings from Tracy to Alice to Frank, each seen alone in the frame, before cutting to close-ups of an increasingly desperate Tracy and a still-confident Frank. Tracy breaks for the window just as the police enter the room, and the movie's climactic chase begins with a shot that anticipates the beginning of *Vertigo* – as did the first shot of *Blackmail,* its abstract wheel prefiguring the abstract line (subsequently identified as a ladder rung) stretching across the *Vertigo* screen.

Again we see a close-up of a whirling wheel, initiating a series of shots that recapitulate the beginning of the film – only this time, views of anxious Alice and desperate Tracy are added to the montage. Tracy's getaway cab is stopped by an ordinary traffic cop (a perfect Hitchcock touch) and, menaced by more policemen on the street, he makes his way on foot to the British Museum. He pauses to drink voraciously from a fountain, using a cup that's attached to the fountain with a chain that drapes over his wrist like a bond or handcuff. The architecture of the building dwarfs Tracy as soon as he comes among the huge pillars of its entryway. Hitchcock films the museum as if it were a surrogate church, with a sense of awe and timelessness; the fountain scene suggests holy water and Tracy's desperate need for salvation. It is very like Hitchcock to find a sense of larger-than-life, almost superhuman power in an architecturally impressive setting that is nonetheless wholly secular in nature.

Tracy walks down a long corridor, receding into the depths of a Hitchcockian tunnel lined with ancient artworks. The large room he comes to also has a tunnel-like conformation, bestowed by a long carpet leading away from the camera into a doorway that Tracy avoids. Huddled in an obscure spot, he watches the reflected images of police rushing by – the illusory again mingling with the real – then makes a break for safety with uniformed cops right behind him. This is followed by one of the film's most justly celebrated, and effectively haunting, shots: Tracy slithering down a rope past a huge, impassive face carved in stone, which presides over the image as a clear surrogate for the impassively observing filmmaker (Fig. 3). It also echoes the mask we saw hanging in Crewe's studio, and evokes the God whose presence might be literally felt if this were indeed a church.

The chase continues down a long corridor, whereupon we cut abruptly to a circular formation, visually startling after the linear shapes that have dominated the screen. Tracy makes his way past a triangular railing, climbs a ladder that's starkly linear, and emerges in the most aggressively circular and convex setting of all – the enormous (and distinctly breastlike) roof of

Figure 3. The great stone face: Tracy (Donald Calthrop) flees past the mask's impassive gaze in *Blackmail*. (Museum of Modern Art/Film Stills Archive)

the building. The ladder climb again anticipates *Vertigo,* while the sight of Tracy and police scaling the curved roof (in long shot) anticipates *Saboteur.* Tracy calls out that he is not the killer, implores the other policemen to ask Frank about the crime, and crashes through a glass skylight before reaching the end of his accusation. It appears that Crewe's death will be blamed forever on him.

Alice, however, has just written a note declaring her intention of turning herself in so that Tracy will not be punished for her deed. The film's symmetrical structure grows as she arrives at New Scotland Yard and confronts the same cop who whispered a joke to her early in the movie. He makes her fill out a form, recalling the bureaucratic rigmarole we've seen in the police station before, and her written words – that her visit concerns the killing – fill the screen as the cop pulls the paper suddenly toward the camera. Alice gazes through a large, light-filled window as he stands before her and speculates on what she has to reveal, reacting to her admission that she's going to tell "who did it" with an ambivalent chuckle.

She walks down another long corridor before entering the chief's office, where Frank has already arrived. He is visibly ill at ease and wonders aloud whether Alice's visit is "worthwhile" now that "everything's been cleared up." The chief is willing to hear her; the lengthy shot moves from one character to another during this agonizing moment, just as it did when Frank, Tracy, and Alice were together just before the chase – linking the characters through an avoidance of cutting, yet isolating them as individuals within the frame. At one point the chief's hand enters the edge of a shot just as Tracy's hand (thrusting money at Frank) did earlier.

The phone rings, distracting the chief's attention before Alice can make her confession. In a new shot – after the chief tells Frank to "deal with this young lady" – she and Frank leave the room. The camera swings between them and another cop outside the office. They find a moment of privacy (a cop presides over the scene, but a glass door prevents him from hearing their words) and Alice tells Frank, for the first time, what happened in Crewe's flat. Locked in a tight two-shot, they walk away from the chief's office, then recede from the camera. Again a hallway indicates the sort of emotional and psychological transition that poses such a challenge to the main characters. Alice stands between Frank and the uniformed cop as he makes his final joke, asking if she told "who did it" and warning Frank that she'll take his job from him. They all laugh – the cop heartily, Frank forcedly, Alice despairingly.

Then something captures Alice's gaze, and (as the cop jokes more about "lady detectives") we cut to a close-up of the laughing-jester painting. A functionary carries it through a doorway, evidently heading for some storage area; we also catch a glimpse of Alice's nude sketch being carried behind it – potentially incriminating, yet unnoticed by all concerned. The film ends with the paintings being carried away from the camera, through a door and down a last hallway, as the sound track rings with the loud, rude laughter of the two men.

Brill notes that many Hitchcock films end with lovers united in the presence of policemen, and associates this not-so-primal scene with "the movement from social rejection to social authorization."[9] Relevant films include *Young and Innocent,* in which Erica's county-constable father shows his approval of the man she has chosen; *Saboteur,* in which a policeman helps Barry away from danger and into his girlfriend's embrace; and *The 39 Steps,* in which the lovers join hands under the eyes of the police. Brill adds *To Catch a Thief* to the list, noting that a police car brings Francie to John for their final handshake and kiss; and it might be observed that Francie's mother – comically invoked at the very end of the film – herself has, in an amusing way, policelike qualities. An extended list might also include films in which lovers come together (or fail to do so) in the presence of authority figures who are not police officers: Scottie's final view of Judy under the eyes of a nun in *Vertigo,* for example, and young Charlie talking with her detective-boyfriend as an unseen clergyman delivers an ironically misconceived eulogy in *Shadow of a Doubt.*

This makes a resonant context for the end of *Blackmail,* in which the police are emphatically present and the lovers are definitely united, but do not embrace or express any sort of affection. Frank certainly loves Alice; he has jeopardized his career and put his integrity into question by concealing the evidence of a killing she committed. And while she has clearly felt flirtatious urges toward other men, these urges have presumably been chased out of her (for the moment, at least) by her traumatic experience in Crewe's studio. Yet the end of the film stresses not affection between the young couple, but rather the moral and emotional ambiguity of their situation. Although the police can be said to connote social authorization here, it's an authorization not fully due to Frank and Alice, whose deeds have been highly dubious from a moral perspective – if not the actual "crime," which was committed in self-defense, then certainly the cover-up and the effort to pin the killing on a man who, however creepy he unquestionably is, hasn't killed anyone.

The last on-screen moments of Alice and Frank are presided over not only by the spirit of the police, in whose headquarters the couple begin and end their story, but by two specific figures. One is the unnamed cop we saw at the beginning of the story, a man prone to mysterious laughter. (We never hear the joke that prompts his first laugh, and his last laugh seems more long and hearty than its motivation would justify.) The other figure is the jester in the painting, whose laugh is less mirthful, more enigmatic, and infinitely longer lasting than the cop's. Under the eyes of these two figures, and under the circumstances they themselves are in, Alice and Frank have all they can do to retain their composure, much less embrace and celebrate their deliverance from danger. It's a striking way for a movie to end; films usually seem more resolved than this, even if Hitchcock often allows daunting questions to linger. The scene indicates his deep interest in states of moral ambiguity and his willingness to manifest them (even this early in his career) through corresponding states of narrative ambivalence.

A final word must be added about the performances in *Blackmail,* which are always solid and sometimes brilliant, especially given the film's status as a pioneering effort in sound cinema. Two deserve special mention. One is the portrayal of Alice by Anny Ondra, who posed a particular challenge when *Blackmail* became a talkie in midproduction. Ondra was a Czechoslovakian actress, and while her Eastern European accent didn't matter as long as the picture was being shot as a silent, everyone agreed that it wouldn't do for a thoroughly English character in a talkie. Another actress, Joan Barry, was therefore recruited to speak Alice's lines from a position just outside camera range – a solution that testifies again to the resourcefulness of Hitchcock's thinking in novel circumstances.

Critics have disagreed on how successfully the arrangement works. There are times, especially in early scenes, when Ondra's body language seems to reflect lip synching rather than acting. Tania Modleski finds political significance in the situation, moreover, calling the movie "uncannily prophetic, anticipating all those sound films for decades to come in which women are more spoken than speaking."[10] Ondra looks so right for the part, however, and her face is so expressive at key moments that she seems altogether suitable. Donald Calthrop, as Tracy, delivers his lines in an oddly patrician accent that's not at all the cockney whine or backcountry drawl that one might expect (in the movies, at least) from such a seemingly lowlife character. His pathetic attempts to placate Frank and Alice and get the police off his tail are among the most squirmingly effective moments in Hitchcock's early work: "I'm not a bad fellow, really" and "A fellow's got to live, you know" are lines that ooze with bitter desperation, especially when contrasted with the threats that Tracy utters in almost the same breath.

Notes

1. Donald Spoto, *The Art of Alfred Hitchcock: Fifty Years of His Motion Pictures.* New York: Hopkinson & Blake, 1977, p. 18.
2. Donald Spoto, *The Dark Side of Genius: The Life of Alfred Hitchcock.* Boston: Little, Brown, 1983, p. 117.
3. François Truffaut, with the collaboration of Helen G. Scott, *Hitchcock.* New York: Simon & Schuster, 1984, p. 61.

4. Ibid., p. 109.

5. Lesley Brill, *The Hitchcock Romance: Love and Irony in Hitchcock's Films.* Princeton, N.J.: Princeton University Press, 1988, p. 147.

6. Brill, *The Hitchcock Romance,* p. 155, says the lyric is "Miss Of-Today," and this may be correct; it's hard to tell.

7. Truffaut, *Hitchcock,* p. 69. Hitchcock calls this moment "a sort of farewell to silent pictures," since in them "the villain was generally a man with a mustache."

8. Leonard J. Leff, *Hitchcock and Selznick: The Rich and Strange Collaboration of Alfred Hitchcock and David O. Selznick in Hollywood.* New York: Weidenfeld & Nicolson, 1987, p. 11.

9. Brill, *The Hitchcock Romance,* p. 28.

10. Tania Modleski, *The Women Who Knew Too Much: Hitchcock and Feminist Theory.* New York: Methuen, 1988, p. 21. Modleski's chapter on *Blackmail* is appropriately called "Rape vs. Mans/laughter." It should be noted that Alice herself, quite apart from the issue of the Ondra/Barry performance, is often "more spoken than speaking," especially during the long scene with Frank and Tracy, during which Frank controls her so thoroughly that even Tracy (who has good reason to war her guilt-ridden words spoken out) complains.

3
Shadow of a Doubt

UNCLE CHARLIE: . . . if you ripped the fronts off houses. . . .

Hitchcock the manipulator presides over many important moments in *Black-mail*, but his more mischievous twin dominates *Shadow of a Doubt* – Hitchcock the joker, the trickster, the prestidigitator. This doesn't mean the film has less serious overtones; indeed, *Shadow of a Doubt* features one of Hitchcock's more heinous villains and unleashes him against an entire family of ostentatiously (if deceptively) wholesome townspeople. But the prospect of a morally intense struggle between good and evil rarely leads Hitchcock to pull in his reins and put on his Sunday face. He's full of tricks and surprises in *Shadow of a Doubt,* and he's as likely to pull them on behalf of wicked Uncle Charlie as to favor the seemingly virtuous heroine of the tale.

The film begins with an opening credit sequence that's more lilting than one might expect, given the subject of the film and the "master of the macabre" reputation that Hitchcock had acquired by 1943. As the credits roll, the screen is filled with couples dancing (in a vertiginous double motion) to the *Merry Widow* waltz, played by a full orchestra with a stately inflection. They will return several times in the course of the film, creating what James McLaughlin calls "a disturbance of the narrative flow that is very unusual in a film of the forties"[1] – a statement that underestimates the narrative complexities of some 1940s cinema (including much of the noir cycle) but calls attention to the function of these images as a classic (and very noirlike) example of the return of repressed material, erupting from an obscure but threatening past into a troubled and tormented present. The unexpected, masquelike presence of the dancers also signals the active presence of Hitchcock in his most manipulative mood.

The first image after the credits is less exotic: a bridge stretching across a river and connoting, like all bridges, an act of reaching out and connecting. Bridges are not uncommon in Hitchcock's iconography, often with positive connotations. Lesley W. Brill notes a moment in *The Lodger,* for example, when the title character and Daisy face each other over a small table behind which "the arch of a fireplace rainbows between the two players and expresses . . . a joining, a coming together"; Brill then conjoins this "symbol of lovers' concord" with a bridge arch in *Secret Agent* and an arched door in *Saboteur.*[2] Bridges and arches may also connote less felicitous moods and possibilities, however – in *The Birds,* for instance, when Melanie passes a picture of the Golden Gate Bridge in the opening shot. In *Shadow of a Doubt* bridging suggests more than one sinister meaning, from the "connection" between Santa Rosa and Uncle Charlie (the former presumably innocent, the latter emphatically evil) to the telepathic link between Uncle Charlie and his young namesake.

The opening left-to-right pan dissolves into a second, similar shot displaying a junkyard with wrecked cars in the foreground, the skyline of a city (Philadelphia) in the background, and what appears to be a roller coaster in the midground. Already, with great economy, Hitchcock is sketching the themes of the story to come. The bridge prefigures certain connections, as noted. The junkyard suggests the desolation of the villain's soul and, more subtly, the desolation of bourgeois family, cultural, and economic life that will be shrewdly criticized in the film. The roller coaster speaks for itself – coming from a filmmaker who likes nothing better than putting his characters, his audience, and his own talents on a wild ride.

The scene then becomes more domesticated. In fact, the movie looks downright ordinary for a few moments, like the work of some *un*mischievous Hitchcock who's taken the prestidigitator's place. More is going on than meets the eye at first, however. The shots of children playing ball indirectly rhyme with the bridge motif, since they involve throwing and running across distances. More important, they remind us that such youngsters signify not just the "innocence" of youth for Hitchcock, but anarchy and even chaos – *vide* the children playing near a crime scene in *Blackmail* or the chanting children of *The Birds* and *Marnie.* The kids give way to an oddly canted view of an apartment house, then an equally canted close-up of one window, and then the star of our story: Uncle Charlie lying on his bed.

He could be sick or paralyzed – spiritually, he will turn out to be both

– since his body is supine except for one forearm, erect at his side. Only his fingers move, toying with a Freudian/Hitchcockian cigar. The camera tracks forward, then pans slightly left, showing a pile of cash in disarray on a small table and more money spilled onto the floor. A cut moves our vantage point to the other side of the room, looking across Charlie and his cigar toward the door, which opens to reveal a stout, middle-aged woman.

Although the narrative is just beginning, Hitchcock the prestidigitator (by our side all the while) has clearly signaled that this quiet, composed, eminently laid-back gentleman is a monster. The main clue, given the film's obviously bourgeois milieu, is that he doesn't take proper care of his money – of which he has plenty, and with which any self-respecting American ought to be deeply concerned (Fig. 4). We don't have time to ponder the meaning of this, because his landlady arrives, but one possibility is easy to imagine: that his indifference to money signals a profound apathy toward everything in and of the world, extending to his own most intimate concerns. (Among other things, the money represents excrement not properly disposed of – that is, not contained and hidden, but left heedlessly in public for all to see, a situation that will reach major prominence in *Psycho*.) Later in the film, this attitude will astound the local bank president, who embodies "normal" capitalist impulses. For now, it indicates that Uncle Charlie is an unnatural creature lying dormant, waiting for the right moment to come alive.

He doesn't stir from his affectless state for the ensuing conversation with his landlady, even when she rushes forward to tidy up his cash. We learn another fact, however, which increases our sense of his unusual nature: "Friends" want to meet with him, yet these "friends" have never seen his face. After the landlady animates him by pulling down the blind – he rises stiffly, like a vampire from his coffin – he expresses rage by flinging a glass toward the sink in his room. Then he lifts the blind to observe his two visitors outside and leaves the room, the camera lingering on his departing shadow in the hallway.

Outdoors, he walks past the visitors, and when they follow him, he escapes them in a remarkable way that has deep implications for the movie to follow: He breezes out of their sight (and out of Hitchcock's, the camera's, and ours) as if he could fly. The camera stays on his pursuers as they vainly look for him; then it pans left and discovers him on a rooftop, barely hidden from the people seeking him, chuckling softly at their bafflement. It's easy to empathize with his delight, and the movie does just that, with a clarinet's quick laugh on the sound track.

It's a clever escape, but also an unexplained one. There are two ways of accounting for Hitchcock's decision to rely on visual sleight of hand rather than

54

Figure 4. Money as metaphor: Uncle Charlie (Joseph Cotten) perplexes the townsfolk in *Shadow of a Doubt*. (Museum of Modern Art/Film Stills Archive. Copyright © by Universal City Studios, Inc. Courtesy of MCA Publishing Rights, a division of MCA, Inc.)

narrative logic at this point. One is his fondness for narrative swiftness at the beginning of a film. The other, more interesting explanation is that Uncle Charlie – like many a character in many a Hitchcock film – has access to cinematic resources not granted to others, bestowed on him with cheerful audacity by a filmmaker who's rarely hesitant to stack the narrative deck in favor of a character (killers included!) that takes his fancy. Neither he nor his camera is in league with Uncle Charlie, but both recognize him as the driving force behind the film. As the focus of its visual and verbal strategies, he has privileges not available to ordinary mortals – privileges that operate exclusively on a cinematic level and indicate his specialness within the world of the story.

Far from being shy about exercising his manipulative powers so overtly, moreover, Hitchcock does it again and again – sometimes for Uncle Charlie, as when he proves unexpectedly absent from his bedroom, and sometimes for Uncle Charlie's foes, as at the climax when young Charlie wins the fight despite her uncle's clear physical advantages. Camerawork also comments on characters in ways that don't play directly into the narrative, as when carvings on the headboard of Uncle Charlie's bed (in what is normally his niece's room) add the outline of wings to his body, shaping him into an angel of death. And let us note once more that none of these practices are unique to *Shadow of a Doubt,* but constitute a key thread running through Hitchcock's oeuvre, wherein tricks and tropes and all manner of interventions – from the sly to the outrageous, from the sneaky to the self-congratulatory, from the artfully inspired to the wistfully attention grabbing – are a central part of the show.

Hitchcock's conjuring continues without pause after Uncle Charlie's rooftop chuckle. The film dissolves to Uncle Charlie sending a telegram, informing his family that he's coming for a visit. ("Try and stop me," he says with uproarious irony.) An important member of this family, the daughter who shares Uncle Charlie's name, is then introduced by Hitchcock in a way that conspicuously echoes our first encounter with her uncle: We see the window of her room from a similarly canted angle; then we see her lying on a bed, supine and paralyzed like him, except that her arms are open in a suggestion of receptivity, in contrast to Uncle Charlie's phallic cigar-play. These visual parallels prepare us for mental connections between the Charlies – connections that become apparent when young Charlie expresses her longing for Uncle Charlie's presence, and reveal their preternatural depth when Uncle Charlie's telegram arrives just as she is preparing to send *him* one. In addition to conventional family affection, there is a tinge of incestuousness to the Charlie–Charlie relationship. This is treated in the wholly indirect way necessary to a mainstream film of the Production Code period, but its repressed presence serves as a narrative "shadow" that envelops the movie's content.

That content unfolds in Santa Rosa, a thoroughly "normal" American community with an old-fashioned sense of law and decency. Its priorities are symbolized by the policeman who directs traffic there: He's a highly visible control figure meant to personify social order, and specifically the limited kind of order that is achieved (or at least aspired to) by human agency. In his ineffectuality he resembles many Hitchcock policemen, such as the cops near the killing scenes in *Blackmail* and *Rope.* His visual prominence in the community gives an utterly false idea of his usefulness. (This heightens the irony later, when Uncle Charlie attains a position of respect in Santa Rosa despite his horrifically evil nature.)

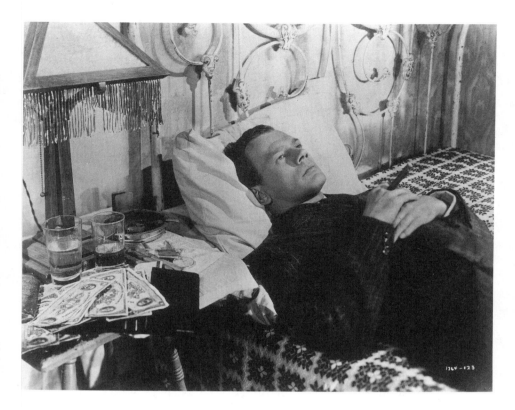

Figure 5. Uncle Charlie as vampire: Joseph Cotten in *Shadow of a Doubt*. (Museum of Modern Art/Film Stills Archive. Copyright © by Universal City Studios, Inc. Courtesy of MCA Publishing Rights, a division of MCA, Inc.)

Unlike the traffic cop, who is painfully typical of the community that employs him, Uncle Charlie is a creature set apart from the common run of humanity – a fact signified by the vampire references that follow him through the film. He is like a vampire in his coffin when first seen, waiting for the sun to sink below the horizon so he can begin his evil activities (Fig. 5). When the landlady draws the blind on his window, her action is traced by the movement of shadow down his face, in a shot that could have been borrowed from a Universal or Hammer horror film. Other signs include his refusal to be photographed and Saunders's half-joking request for Ann to tell "the story of Dracula" as they walk away from church on a Sunday morning. McLaughlin notes even more: young Charlie's remark that she and her uncle "have the same blood," Uncle Charlie's superstrong grip and origins in "the East," and the

57

fundamental fact that his niece mentally "summons" him to her waiting and willing side.

The vampire references of *Shadow of a Doubt* are woven into the narrative with typically Hitchcockian relish. This film is one of his most incisive attempts to explore horrors and instabilities lurking just below the seemingly controlled surfaces of "average" American life, and he was clearly delighted with the suitability of the Dracula/Nosferatu myth to the metaphorical aspects of this project. Indeed, another great filmmaker made similar use of the same myth just three years later: Orson Welles, whose 1946 thriller *The Stranger* has so many parallels with *Shadow of a Doubt* that it's worth pausing to consider the films together for a moment.

The relationship between Hitchcock and Welles is complex; each artist seems to have felt the other's influence more than once – one thinks of the carnivalesque climaxes in *The Lady from Shanghai* (1948) and *Strangers on a Train* (1951) and of Janet Leigh victimized by hotel-room voyeurism in *Touch of Evil* (1958) as well as *Psycho* (1960). The link between *Shadow* and *Stranger* is the strongest, though, including the following similarities:

1. Uncle Charlie and the disguised Nazi of Welles's film, Kindler/Rankin, are both compared visually with vampires.
2. Both men have successfully avoided being photographed.
3. Both find that their secrets have fallen into the hands of a woman; both women fail to go to the authorities, even when an authority is nearby and eager to be gone to; both villains try to murder the women by sawing through a stairway or ladder.
4. Both films suggest telepathic links between good and bad individuals: in *Shadow* between the Charlies; in *Stranger* between Kindler/Rankin and the American agent pursuing him.
5. Both films show not only individuals but whole communities in linked or parallel terms. The transitions to California and Connecticut (in the respective films) are handled in similar ways; both towns have large churches where key scenes take place; both towns have control figures (the traffic cop in *Shadow*, the town clerk in *Stranger*) who play small roles in the action but occupy important places in the mise-en-scène.
6. Both films have film noir characteristics but eschew noir's usual urban setting, instead picturing smaller communities as infected, traplike places.

The presence of so many parallels must indicate a strong connection not only between the two films, but between them and the mood of the mid–1940s period when they appeared. This was a time of war and insecurity for the United States, where Hitchcock had by then ensconced himself. Since he had long considered family life to be a mental, moral, and emotional battleground, it is not surprising that he chose the bourgeois home to embody – in addition to his darkling view of personal interactions – socially and politically inflected tensions not unlike those he explored more directly in *Saboteur* the year before and *Lifeboat* the year after.

Shadow of a Doubt may be considered an exploration and indictment of the increasingly chaotic nature of American life during this period. In ways, it seems even more despairing than the war-related dramas just mentioned, since it inscribes the incipient psychoses of American life in "ordinary" citizens without recourse to treacherous Nazis or hostile foreign powers. To accompmplish this, Hitchcock employs the sort of nightmarish plot and shadowy visuals that are two of film noir's most consistently encountered traits, and the horror-film conventions already discussed, which have strong resonances on political, cultural, and psychoanalytic levels.

Shadow of a Doubt refers to the vampire-movie tradition with surprising frequency. Uncle Charlie is like a vampire on the narrative as well as the visual level – an alien invader whose very presence contaminates the environment wherein he operates and threatens to corrupt others, especially those he chooses as targets. His activities also have the heavy overlay of sexual aggression that is common to the vampire genre. His criminal career involved marrying each victim before murdering her, and we have already noted the incestuous overtones in his relationship with his niece. Young Charlie longs (lusts?) for Uncle Charlie to enter her home and terminate the lethargy (linked with middle-class family life) that envelops her; henceforth, she needs rescuing from his loathsome clutches as surely as any of the incrementally vampirized women in Dracula movies. Hitchcock also draws on the vampire-film tradition in matters of imagery and montage (Fig. 6).

The film's narrative is built largely around the Charlie–Charlie relationship. This links *Shadow of a Doubt* with the common noir motif of a "spider woman" (itself recalling Hitchcock's frequent guilty-woman theme) who tempts and ensnares a male victim. Although she is ostensibly innocent and even virtuous, young Charlie indeed calls for her uncle, if on a semiconscious and telepathic level that bypasses ordinary experience and understanding; and to the extent that she is "responsible" for his arrival in Santa Rosa, she may be said to have inflicted his evil presence on her entire family – especially her father, who suffers disproportionately from the belittlement and displacement that Uncle Charlie visits on him.

Another noir motif, which may be considered complementary to that of the spider woman, is that of a person (generally male) who poses in a

59

Figure 6. Fearful symmetry: Young Charlie (Teresa Wright) felled by Uncle Charlie (Joseph Cotten) in *Shadow of a Doubt*. (Museum of Modern Art/ Film Stills Archive. Copyright © by Universal City Studios, Inc. Courtesy of MCA Publishing Rights, a division of MCA, Inc.)

household and/or community under a false identity with an assumed set of behaviors. Hitchcock liked this device, particularly during the 1940s high-noir period; it characterizes not only *Shadow of a Doubt,* with its serial killer posing as a lovable family man, but also *Rope,* with its Nietzsche-quoting murderers hosting a seemingly pleasant middle-class party, and *Notorious,* with its (female) operative marrying a Nazi for purposes of espionage. On a political level, the motif has a clear allegorical function: Persons of repugnant (or simply different) views may enter a household or community and dwell there unsuspected, biding their time until the right conditions for action arrive. The vampire myth is a ready-made metaphor for this situation.

Since these matters crop up in more than one film during this period, including *The Stranger,* they call for historical and sociological examination.

One illuminating perspective is suggested by Warren I. Susman's idea that an important sociological change took place in the United States during the early decades of the twentieth century: from a popular emphasis on the notion of *character* (manifested in such qualities as duty, honor, morals, manners, integrity, manhood) to an emphasis on *personality* (reflected by such adjectives as fascinating, magnetic, masterful, dominant). Popular "personality" literature is steeped in notions about cultivating charm, projecting an influential aura, and learning correct formulas of dress, body language, and so forth.[3]

Uncle Charlie is a superb, if hyperbolic embodiment of the difference between character and personality. He subverts all duty and honor in his psychotic, self-assigned mission as an "avenging angel," manifesting not a shred of moral integrity. When the clergyman in the last scene eulogizes people like Uncle Charlie by saying, "their sterling characters... the sweetness of their characters live on with us forever," the emptiness of his words is heavily ironic.

At the same time, Uncle Charlie carves out a false yet persuasive identity by flaunting proper mannerisms of speech, clothing, gesture, and above all, the sort of "family values" that have become standard issue for everyone from demagogues to pop psychologists. All surface and no substance, except for the core of evil that glows deep within him, he might be called "a shadow, a mere chaos of appearances," to borrow a phrase from Jorge Luis Borges's 1945 review of *Citizen Kane*.[4] In yet another irony, however, he is abetted in his project by the gullibility of his personality-hungry family – including young Charlie, who tries desperately to believe in him, remaining quiet even after his guilt is unquestionable. On the level of pure technique, one can imagine a Dale Carnegie celebrating Uncle Charlie, who goes from loathsome murderer to friend-winning and people-influencing pillar of the community through sheer force of personality.

Matters like these were on people's minds during the mid–1940s period, which Susman labels not only the "Age of Anxiety" but also the "Age of Jung" because of its concern with myth and the collective unconscious.[5] This period led to the late 1940s and 1950s, moreover, when concepts of "personal identity" became a key preoccupation. It is not surprising that an age of both anxiety and Jung would give a Hitchcock the inspiration to drape middle-class family life with mythic *Dracula* overtones, or that the imminence of a personal-identity era would give a personality-flaunter like Uncle Charlie the opportunity to flourish. (Nor is *Shadow of a Doubt* the only film in which Hitchcock shows an awareness of character/personality complexities; e.g., see *Suspicion* [1941], where Lina McLaidlaw is described as having "intellect and a fine solid character," yet kisses Johnny Aysgarth in a willed display of the personality she would like to have.)

As noted, Hitchcock exposes the nature of Uncle Charlie's true character – even while his personality continues to deceive people in the film – partly through vampire imagery. By using this imagery as an exteriorized (hence visible) representation of Uncle Charlie's inwardly evil nature, Hitchcock employs a process fundamental to the horror film throughout its history. Thomas Elsaesser sheds light on this in his suggestion that uncanny film creatures and powers may be seen as consequences of pressures generated by "social and political moments."[6] Hitchcock engages in sociopolitical criticism with great subtlety in *Shadow of a Doubt*, not using a *literal* vampire character as a symbolic *substitute* for the social and political moment – that is, the turbulent early 1940s, as experienced by the American middle class – but rather *adding* vampire-related elements (shadows, telepathy, suggestions of demonic powers, etc.) to his depiction of a seemingly genuine (albeit very evil) mortal who indeed personifies the worst tendencies of that moment.

The result is a depiction of Uncle Charlie and his sociopolitical period that imbues them with horror (via monster-related imagery) while simultaneously showing them in their cultivated personality guise of normality and virtue. It's true that Hitchcock's strategy shifts many of the horrific signifiers connected with Uncle Charlie slightly away from his own body, locating them externally (shadow, cigar smoke) or giving them a frankly mysterious nature (telepathic power, aversion to cameras). Hitchcock's view of him as a monstrous figure is not compromised, however. Rather, his treatment of Uncle Charlie may be described in terms of what Noël Carroll calls "horrific metonymy," referring to cases where "the horror . . . is not something that can be perceived by the naked eye [but rather] the horrific being is *surrounded* by objects that we antecedently take to be objects of disgust and/or phobia."[7] Many of Uncle Charlie's props, trappings, and trademarks are such "objects."

Another mark of the film's historical specificity is its use of psychoanalytic ideas. Psychoanalysis had a high profile in Hollywood during this period, often figuring in films noirs and in Hitchcock's own work, most notably in *Spellbound*, made two years after *Shadow of a Doubt*. One sees psychoanalytic notions at work in the physical position of both Charlies (recumbent and therefore conductive to fantasy; cf. the Freudian couch) at the beginning of the story;[8] in Uncle Charlie's clear status as a representative of young Charlie's rampant id functions; and in the phallic imagery that plays a major role in the film – from the opening scene, when Uncle Charlie toys with his cigar, to the moment when he meets a phallically inscribed death, falling from a forward-thrusting train after waiting for its movement to attain the proper (climax-producing) tempo for his assault on young Charlie. (For the best evidence of train as phallic symbol in Hitchcock, see the last flamboyant shot of *North by Northwest*.) Also manifested in the film is Freud's notion of the *thanatos* or "death wish" instinct: Uncle Charlie travels to Santa Rosa in a train, as if anticipating – perhaps impatiently, like a typically miserable member of the undead – the destiny that awaits him.

Phallic symbolism constituted during the 1940s (as today) a particularly well known and frequently popularized aspect of psychoanalytic theory, working its way into much popular culture of the period. For all its modern psychologizing, however, *Shadow of a Doubt* returns to a far more primitive level for the final resolution of the struggle between Uncle Charlie and his antagonist – primitive not only in its physicality but also in its magical undertones. Here the film's *Dracula* imagery becomes highly relevant again. Roger Dadoun notes that "all the paraphernalia of fetishism" in vampire films – including the cross, which "brings about a regression to a magic stage" – are effective against the monster insofar as they share "his basic character."[9] The means that Uncle Charlie employs in the definitive attempt to kill his niece (after failed attempts that have frustrated and angered him) are so awful – that is, the speeding train is so powerful, and the prospect of being thrown/crushed/severed is so terrifying – as to reveal more vividly than ever the evilness of his "basic character" and to suggest that it must be defeated by actions that are correspondingly drastic and horrible. Accordingly, he meets precisely the fate that he intended for his niece, a fate conceived in the depths of his "basic character" and inflicted by her as he had meant to inflict it.

The symmetry is even stronger if we see the thrusting train in phallic terms, since Uncle Charlie's vampire-myth characteristics also carry strong phallic implications. Writing of the title character in Murnau's *Nosferatu*, Dadoun suggests that the monster's rigidity and the appearance of his face, ears, fangs, and other features make him a sort of "walking phallus or 'phallambulist,' " adding that he "might be called the Pointed One, bearing in mind all the simple and basic symbolism attached to pointedness."[10] To the extent that Uncle Charlie is a Nosferatu/Dracula doppelgänger, the climax of his story shows one phallic agent meeting another on its own terms.

Shadow of a Doubt is another of Hitchcock's imperfectly, yet unmistakably circular tales, much as *Blackmail* was meant to be. Uncle Charlie arrives on a train and meets his death on one; young Charlie's yearning for a male savior begins with a call for her uncle and ends in her alliance with a detective who hunted the same man for different reasons; Uncle Charlie's deathlike immobility in his first appearance is echoed by true death in his last.

Uniting all this is the supreme circularity resulting from Hitchcock's two most overt interventions into the logic of the narrative – in the opening scene, when he whisks Uncle Charlie away from his pursuers, and at the climax, when young Charlie's victory seems quite gratuitous, since her uncle's superior size and strength (not to mention his vampirelike grip) would seem to ensure *his* triumph in any physical contest. On both occasions, Hitchcock the joker is visible in the narrative almost as plainly as the characters he's so avidly manipulating.

Yet a serious Hitchcock is present too, brooding over the somber implications of the tale. While the giggle of a clarinet greeted Uncle Charlie's first-act escape, his last-act funeral is accompanied by the equally ironic, but far less flippant, sound of a minister's ignorant eulogy and a young woman's vain attempt to find comforting order in an irrational world. Shadows and doubts, indeed.

Notes

1. James McLaughlin, "All in the Family: Alfred Hitchcock's *Shadow of a Doubt*," in *A Hitchcock Reader,* ed. Marshall Deutelbaum and Leland Poague. Ames: Iowa State University Press, 1986, pp. 141–52, cited at 149–50.

2. Lesley W. Brill, "Hitchcock's *The Lodger*," in ibid. pp. 67–77, cited at p. 70.

3. Warren I. Susman, *Culture as History: The Transformation of American Society in the Twentieth Century.* New York: Pantheon, 1985, pp. 271–85.

4. Jorge Luis Borges, "Citizen Kane," originally in *Sur* 83, 1945; reprinted in *Focus on Citizen Kane*, Ronald Gottesman, ed. Englewood Cliffs, N.J.: Prentice-Hall, pp. 127–8, cited at 127.

5. Susman, *Culture as History*, p. 284.

6. Thomas Elsaesser, "Social Mobility and the Fantastic: German Silent Cinema," originally in *Wide Angle* 5:2, 1982; reprinted in *Fantasy and the Cinema*, ed. James Donald. London: BFI Publishing, 1989, pp. 23–38, cited at 31.

7. Noël Carroll, *The Philosophy of Horror, or, Paradoxes of the Heart.* New York: Routledge, 1989, p. 51.

8. Noted by McLaughlin, p. 141.

9. Roger Dadoun, "Fetishism in the Horror Film," originally in *Nouvelle revue de psychanalyse*, Autumn 1970; reprinted in Donald, *Fantasy and the Cinema*, cited at pp. 58–9; trans. by Annwyl Williams.

10. Ibid., pp. 54–5.

4

The Wrong Man

USED CAR DEALER: She look like a wrong one to you?
— *Psycho*

Of all the films Hitchcock made during the 1950s, *The Wrong Man* captures most vividly and chillingly the American spirit of its time. This is not because his other 1950s films try and fail to make social and cultural observations, but because they set out in quest of other goals. Many deal with personal obsessions that tend to cut their protagonists off from the American culture around them: Scottie in *Vertigo* is fixated on his dreams of Judy/Madeleine to the exclusion of virtually all else; Bruno in *Strangers on a Train* is fixated on his murder scheme, and Guy is fixated (not exactly by choice) on Bruno; the characters of *Dial "M" for Murder* are claustrophobically wrapped up in one another's machinations. *I Confess* relates its protagonist to the special environment of the church; *To Catch a Thief* and *The Man Who Knew Too Much* remove their main characters from the American landscape; *The Trouble with Harry* is a pastoral comedy with its own bucolic atmosphere.

Even two films that appear to be exceptions wind up confirming the rule more than they refute it. *Rear Window* presents its protagonist with a microcosm of urban American behavior, but he gives his attention to those aspects that echo his own preoccupations and suspicions; and *North by Northwest* is at once too whimsical, too frenetic, and too peripatetic to be considered a thoroughgoing gloss on the social and cultural phenomena that figure in it – although, as with the other films, a great deal may be deduced regarding the society and culture that *produced* it.

By contrast, *The Wrong Man* seems very much (and very intentionally) a film about the 1950s. While it focuses on some of Hitchcock's most deeply

65

felt personal obsessions, particularly his persistent guilt feelings and his dread of police and authority figures, it places its protagonist squarely in the realm of social interaction, portraying a man in conflict not only with his inner self but also with the society around him – manifested in the forbidding institutions of the criminal-justice system and, more intimately, in the supposedly wholesome and stabilizing institution of the 1950s-style bourgeois family.

Especially revealing in these conflicts is the evidence they provide of sadomasochistic tendencies in the protagonist's mentality and in the social, cultural, and psychological mechanisms of American life in general during this period. Although this is not an explicitly spelled-out theme of the film, it courses through many aspects of the narrative and the visual style – from the assertively bleak mise-en-scène, suggesting a willingly endured alienation that quite contradicts the supposed 1950s ideals of contentment and consensus, to the protagonist's oddly passive stance when faced with bitter assaults on his integrity and freedom. Also relevant to this theme are the film's view of family life as an inadequate yet compulsively embraced haven from a disordered and untrustworthy world, and Hitchcock's characteristically sardonic view of social systems (here the criminal-justice system) as arenas or "theaters" for class-coded mechanisms of social and personal control.

The tug of sadistic and/or masochistic currents can be found elsewhere in Hitchcock's work, as well; *vide* the purposeful inflictions of psychological or physical pain in movies from *Blackmail* to *Rope* to *Frenzy* and the miseries almost eagerly endured by such tormented characters as Lina McLaidlaw in *Suspicion,* Alicia Huberman in *Notorious,* and Scottie Ferguson in *Vertigo.* But nowhere do such currents show more strength or insidiousness than in *The Wrong Man.*

During the 1950s, much of the American cultural apparatus outdid itself in positing and reinforcing an image of the United States as a "new affluent society" that was emblematized most succinctly by "the image of the happy suburban home."[1] Since that time, however, many commentators have disparaged the 1950s as a terribly oppressive decade, characterized by enforced conformity to dubious, yet ferociously defended, social norms.

There is much to support a dim view of this period and its tenacious denial of social and political problems that continued to fester beneath the surface of American life, finally exploding into the open during the 1960s. The 1950s have been a badly underrated decade, however, where certain cultural achievements are concerned. On one hand, it is true that strong sociocultural forces such as suburban migration, industrially co-opted graphic arts, and the growth of television relentlessly promoted carefully circumscribed folkways, mores, and "values." But at the same time, a well-spring of original and subversive artistic activity was bubbling away: The "beat generation" literature of Jack Kerouac and Allen Ginsberg; the jazz of Charlie Parker and Miles Davis; the theater of Julian Beck and Judith Malina; the rock and roll of many doo-wop and rockabilly artists; the art of Jackson Pollock; the television of Ernie Kovacs; and the comic-book pastiches of *Mad* magazine were just a few of its more important eruptions.

Hollywood cinema was less obviously innovative, but in retrospect it is clear that the imminent breakdown of the studio system, coupled with the continuing activity of such old masters as John Ford, Howard Hawks, and others, made for a great deal of dazzling activity. Hitchcock, a certified old master who never tired of new explorations, was in the forefront of this activity; *The Wrong Man,* made and released in 1956, represents his attempt to probe some of the period's least attractive aspects in detail. He accomplishes this by focusing on a man who conforms so heedlessly to the public assumptions of his day that the revolutionary developments of a barely hidden subculture, and its attendant encouragements to think and act for oneself, are for him nonexistent – even though, irony of ironies, that man is himself an artist with daily exposure to part of the New York City jazz scene!

The Wrong Man is based on actual events – detailed in *Life* magazine and in a story treatment that Warner Bros. acquired from the *Life* author – with obvious appeal for Hitchcock, given their combination of mistaken identity and guilt–innocence confusion. The protagonist is Christopher Emmanuel Balestrero/Henry Fonda, a New York dance-band musician who is arrested, arraigned, and tried for a series of holdups he did not commit. He is exonerated when the real thief is caught during another crime, but not before his family shatters and his wife undergoes a mental breakdown.

Parallels with Franz Kafka's *The Trial* are easy to find, as are parallels with Hitchcock's earlier work: not only the confounding of good with evil but also fascination with police procedure (here contemplated in extreme detail) and intense interest in performance as an activity bridging the gap between the true and the illusory. Also present is Hitchcock's concern with physical and moral immobility. In this film he builds an uncommonly elaborate material structure to generate both a state of metaphorical paralysis (actualized most dramatically in the jail-cell episode) that engulfs and stifles the protagonist, and an uncommonly bold metaphysical apparatus (actualized in a prayer and what could be a miracle) that provides a partial and ambiguous release from the paralytic condition.

On its most obvious level, *The Wrong Man* is the story of an innocent person who is mistaken – by the police, several witnesses, and the criminal-justice system at large – for a villain. Hitchcock employed certain documentary-type methods when shooting the film, using black-and-white cinematography and setting various scenes in real locations, including streets of New York City and the ballroom of the Stork Club in Manhattan, where Manny earns his living as a bass player. The film takes further pains to assure us of its authenticity through printed statements and a direct address by Hitchcock to the audience (his most elaborate cameo) vouching for the real-life roots of the story. Although it is obviously a Hollywood drama with recognized performers and a carefully written screenplay, Hitchcock clearly wants us to think of *The Wrong Man* as something of a semi-documentary, or at least a drama possessing more real-life authority than most.

While the film is more of a many-layered achievement than the semi-documentary label suggests, it is worth pausing to consider the implications of documentary style – the use of location shooting, for instance – as this intersects with the primary concerns of Hitchcock's career. From one perspective, all documentary filmmaking may imply a forceful confrontation with the real world. "It can be argued," writes Fred Camper, "that the photographing of any cinema image of a part of the actual world is an act of aggression" since the photographer "wrenches a specific part of reality from the context with which it makes a whole, places that fragment in a rectangular frame, and further delimits it in time."[2]

One might reply, of course, that such photography is equally and alternatively an act of love, tribute, preservation, or any number of other things. But if one carries the aggression hypothesis a little further, another practice in *The Wrong Man* – the use of actual figures from the Balestrero case in minor roles – additionally calls to mind Susan Sontag's statement that to photograph people "is to violate them, by seeing them as they never see themselves, by having knowledge of them they can never have; it turns people into objects that can be symbolically possessed," and that to photograph an individual "is a sublimated murder – a soft murder, appropriate to a sad, frightened time."[3] Such suggestions that aggression may reside in the very act of photography shed light on Hitchcock's affinity for cinema – he was, after all, preoccupied with aggression throughout his filmmaking career – and make it seem logical that he would steer toward the photographic acts of "wrenching, delimiting, violating," and so forth in a real-life context at least once in his career.

The Wrong Man also owes a great deal to traditions very different from documentary, however. One is the German expressionist style, which contributes some of the movie's most obvious tropes, such as a moment when Manny's vertiginous reaction to imprisonment is evoked by a whirling camera movement that couldn't be more removed from standard documentary practice. Another is film noir, itself an amalgamation of German expressionism and other elements. The influence of noir is felt in such major elements of *The Wrong Man* as its shadowy mise-en-scène, its brooding urban landscapes, the labyrinthian set of challenges faced by its protagonist, and (a feature of many nonnoir 1940s and 1950s films as well) its fascination with Freudian psychiatry. Smaller details, such as the importance of telephones in the narrative and mise-en-scène, also recall noir conventions; and the last shot is pure noir, countering an unhappy narrative and ambivalent plot resolution with a tacked-on "happy" ending that couldn't be more deliberately unconvincing.

The concatenation of expressionism, noir, and documentary with Hitchcock's own approach makes for a structure rich in dialogic implications and gives *The Wrong Man* much of its visual resonance. The film also operates strongly as an aural experience, beginning with the credit sequence, when we see people dining and dancing (their evening on the town condensed to a few moments, by dissolves) while Manny plays with the Stork Club band. The music has a significant structure: fully voiced passages alternating with thinly orchestrated interludes. If they came occasionally, these interludes might serve as appealingly whimsical respites from the full passages, but heard with unsparing predictability, they become convulsive lapses into a weak and wan monotony. The stagnant pattern of Manny's life, which we will soon observe for ourselves, is echoed here all too vividly.

The narrative begins when Manny leaves his bass in Manhattan and heads for home in Queens, going through motions that are clearly habitual and ingrained. Being fair to Manny and to the period when the story occurs, it should be noted that most people are governed largely by habit in any time and place, except under exceptional circumstances. What's revealing about Manny's activities is not so much their habitual nature as the evidently unquestioning attitude behind them – he never seems to think critically about his life, even though it doesn't seem very fulfilling in many respects – and the fact that others (especially men) share so many of them.

Manny is less visibly a member of the "lonely crowd" than he might be, since he works at night and hence reverses "normal" work and leisure hours. He reverses them with an exactness that is equally confining, however. He dresses just like others of his class and gender, moreover, and his actions on the way home from work are routinized along social as well as personal lines: travel by subway, food at a particular diner where he eats "the usual" and speaks perfunctorily with the waiter, a pause at the front stoop to gather the morning's milk delivery. The house itself is generic and without distinguishing characteristics. Even his children sleep in identical postures, on ready display for the brief gaze he gives them before entering his own room. His wife, Rose/Vera Miles, turns out to be, not surprisingly, an amalgam of popular-magazine styles and mannerisms.

With bad teeth, however. This flaw confirms what we might have suspected from the conspicuously drab manner in which Hitchcock has filmed our first glimpses of Manny's life: All is not perfect in this world that elicits such flat and dull behavior. A brief conversation reveals a host of troubles, some acute and some chronic, gnawing away at the Balestrero household. Rose's teeth not only ache but will be expensive to treat; the family's financial situation is poor; and every time Manny and Rose begin to find a solid footing, some unexpected problem lands them in debt again. They take pains to reassure each other (and the spectator) of their mutual love and regard, but there is little enthusiasm in their dialogue.

Nor, significantly, is there any suggestion of where they might turn for help. This wouldn't be surprising in a film about very poor or otherwise disadvantaged people. Manny and Rose have attained a certain level in life, however. He is an artist with finely developed skills, employment in a prestigious club, and a steady income; she runs a comfortable home and raises average children. They live in a decent middle-class community and are on good terms with an extended family. Yet despite these solid bourgeois attainments, Rose's impacted teeth loom as a major threat to their happiness.

Even at this early moment in the story, we are able to feel the loneliness – more accurately, the isolation – that is a dominant characteristic of this couple's life. The family unit is their comfort and shelter, but the unit *itself* has no comfort and shelter to which it might resort. Manny's answer to the latest financial crisis – borrowing once more against an insurance policy – is an inward-turning solution that further emphasizes this isolated condition. On the streets of New York, as we have seen, he is an undistinguished figure traveling by rote through unquestioned routines that are replicated by countless others. In his home, we now observe, he and his family have little more in the way of true warmth or satisfaction. For the individual and the family, life is as dull and difficult as Hitchcock's style in this film (bourgeois noir, we might call it) graphically signals it to be.

Still and all, Manny and Rose manage to live under these circumstances without giving way to despair, and no doubt believe they are as happy as ordinary mortals can expect to be. One reason must be their mutual determination to bolster each other's spirits, even at times when the most superficial hope and optimism are not truly felt – an example being Rose's effort to stay smiling and cheerful as she tells Manny about the price tag for her dental work, and denies that her teeth hurt badly. This moment is among the first indications that performance is, again, one of Hitchcock's main concerns in the narrative. In addition, Manny begins the film by performing on his musical instrument, and his children perform by presenting themselves to his gaze as quietly and symmetrically as greeting-card cherubs. He and Rose start acting for each other immediately, stating bleak truths with cheery demeanors. Cracks soon appear in the facade, as when Manny grimaces at the actual cost of the dental work; but soon it's back to smiles, reassurances, and strained facsimiles of contentment.

I don't mean to suggest that Manny and Rose are not happy in many ways with each other, their home, and their relationship. The human condition is a difficult one, and middle-class respectability is not the worst means yet devised for coping with it. Hitchcock does not seek to demolish his characters or their way of life in the name of cultural criticism. What he does seek to demolish is complacency, here manifested in the *assumption* that middle-class virtues and behaviors will bring fulfillment and contentment in their wake, and in the *willingness* to endure various difficulties that are felt to be necessary aspects of bourgeois living. Manny and Rose have done everything "right." Yet they are dogged by uncertainty and decay, symbolized by the festering tooth problems that plague Rose and (we later learn) have tormented Manny, too. Hitchcock's project is neither to moralize about nor to rectify their situation, but rather to exacerbate it until its most desperate extremities have been exposed for all, including the protagonists, to see.

His other project, which occupies much of the film, is to examine particular aspects of the bleakness and isolation that are endemic to Manny's sociocultural milieu. Hitchcock accomplishes this through the confrontation between Manny and the criminal-justice system – the very sector of American society that should (according to its claims) be the strength and protection of Manny's class. As the foundation of this system – and of its ability to elicit the cooperation not only of its clear beneficiaries, but also of its potential victims, such as Manny himself – Hitchcock posits a complex series of mechanisms that require control-oriented behaviors by people who belong to some social strata, and submission-oriented behaviors by those deemed to occupy lower levels. The dynamics of control and submission (congruent with sadism and masochism, in psychoanalytic terms) take the form of theatrical behaviors – a familiar Hitchcock conceit, here used to explore not only the boundaries of truth and illusion in terms of personal psychology, but also the operations of domination and defeat in society at large and in the family as society's microcosm.

Surely reflecting his own responses to the sociocultural ethos of the 1950s, Hitchcock's work during this decade shows a special incisiveness with regard to theatrical behavior – and particularly to directorial behavior, whereby a dominating person assumes a measure of control over an individual who is at least momentarily submissive. (In exploring directorial behavior, Hitchcock leans toward cinematics rather than stagecraft as his key metaphor, since cinema more strongly privileges the director's role.) The most extreme example is Scottie in *Vertigo,* who "casts" Judy in the role of Madeleine and arranges her costume, appearance, and so forth. The conflict in *Strangers on a Train* grows largely from Guy's refusal to follow Bruno's direction; Logan's predicaments in *I Confess* stem from his role in the church's centuries-old production; Wendice "casts" Lesgate as a killer in *Dial "M" for Murder;* spies and government agents "cast" Thornhill as Kaplan in *North by Northwest;* and so on.

The Wrong Man is filled with directors. The police take on this function with special enthusiasm, casting Manny in the role of holdup man (before any official accusation has been brought against him) and sending him into stores, where he puts on an apparently gripping performance simply by walking around for a moment. In one case the store's proprietor also starts directing Manny, having him remove his hat and repeat his movements. (Robert Stam observes that the film is "informed in its entirety" by a verbal pun translated into visual/narrative terms, since Manny "plays bass" for a living and "plays base" when mimicking the actions of a criminal.[4]) At the police station a little later, Manny asks why he is being treated as he is, and the policeman's answer synthesizes the issues of performance (a certain "procedure" must be followed) and social ritual (it's all a "routine" matter) that are among Hitchcock's greatest preoccupations during this period of his career.

The sense of theatricality and movieness grows stronger as Manny comes more firmly under police control, culminating in the two lineup scenes. In the first, Manny assumes his place "onstage" while the lieutenant coaches

Figure 7. Sound stage: Manny (Henry Fonda) on display in *The Wrong Man*. (© 1957 Warner Bros. Pictures Inc.; renewed 1984 Warner Bros. Inc.; all rights reserved. Museum of Modern Art/Film Stills Archive.)

two witnesses in their role as identifiers, which they play to the hilt by identifying our innocent hero. In the second (Fig. 7), Manny steps onto a "sound stage" complete with a microphone and an officious "director" on a nearby platform, who looks for all the world like Cecil B. DeMille supervising his latest epic. Still later, Manny plays a scene in court, and once again the controlling system has been set up in such a way that the performer can carry an unfamiliar role by following the path of least resistance through a ritualized procedure – in this case, standing mute while a supporting player (a defense attorney who appears from nowhere) speaks his lines for him. Everyone tries to direct Manny, right down to his mother – who gives him instructions for praying – and the psychiatric nurse who coaches him during his last visit with his wife; revealingly, Rose has more resistance and proves less tractable than her sane husband.

73

That sanitorium scene points up a key fact about Manny and his malleability: He takes to all this direction as if he hungered for it. This characteristic is what makes him Hitchcock's most savage paradigm for the 1950s – a socially conditioned "organization man" so lonely for a crowd that he's willing to cooperate with even the most hostile institution if it offers him the submissive security of a structured role to play.

Is it unfair to suggest that Manny might reject these roles, and the attentions of the police who foist the most outrageous roles on him? Not if one judges him by the same standard that applies to Joseph K. in *The Trial*. Kafka's accused and arrested K. is informed that he need not fear the court system if he is innocent but can freely leave and return to his normal life – something K. refuses to do, constantly revealing his guilt by insisting on one more appearance, one more legal brief, one more consultation with one more official. Manny's behavior is strikingly similar. From the first, his attitude toward Lieutenant Bowers and the other policemen is one of quiet submission. He accompanies them with hardly a murmur, failing even to step through his front door and inform his wife about what's going on. He tells them what they want to know without questioning their authority to ask or the necessity of their particular inquiries. He calls everyone "sir" and strains to cooperate with the most humiliating demands, such as the forced parades through recently robbed establishments. He calls his own lawyer "Mr. O'Connor" while the attorney calls him by his first name. (An authority figure in Manny's eyes, and therefore wise in all things, O'Connor must even perceive and point out Rose's degenerating mental condition before Manny can take notice of it.)

His actions could be deemed irrational if not for two available (and complementary) explanations:

1. Manny is the product of a masochistically inclined time when conformity is seen as a virtue in itself and when entire lives are given over to endorsing, through participation, a set of rigidly defined social norms that include cooperation with authority regardless of personal cost.[5]
2. Manny is guilty, guilty, guilty – not of the crimes he is charged with, of course, but of failing to surmount his submissive impulses, of failing to overcome a deep malaise that informs his life, of failing to avoid a perception of decay in the middle-class existence he has attempted to order so thoroughly.

At a time when "procedure" and "routine" are supposedly surefire keys to personal and societal success, his uneasy feelings of discontent make him seem (probably to others and surely to himself) a social traitor. He suppresses these discontents before and during his criminal-justice ordeal, allowing only an occasional sign to slip through, such as that grimace at the news of Rose's dental costs. Yet the hidden misery of the Balestrero household makes itself felt in other ways – most dramatically in Rose's breakdown, which significantly fails to go away even when Manny's immediate crisis has ended, and in Hitchcock's overarching directorial style, with its noir starkness and bursts of expressionistic excess. As hero of the film and his 1950s family, Manny was supposed to make things nice by submitting to convention at every opportunity and following every available rule, physically and emotionally. He has obviously failed, especially in the emotion department, despite his best efforts.

His efforts are impressive, though, resulting in a many-faceted performance. For his own benefit, he plays a proper (and properly self-deluding) personality of the 1950s. For his family, he plays a competent provider and companion who has fallen on bad luck and hard times. For the police, he plays a submissive pawn in a socially determined spectacle. Meanwhile, he is also performing for Hitchcock, who isn't shy about asserting his own control when the performance threatens to veer "out of character." For instance, only once does Manny raise his voice to the police, during his interrogation in the precinct station. Lieutenant Bowers shows no anger at Manny's outburst, but bends before it, agreeing to reveal the facts behind his arrest – whereupon Hitchcock cuts to a sudden (and startling) high-angle shot that signals his participation in the policeman's "nice cop" gambit *and* reminds us of his ultimate control over all components of the narrative.

Asserting complicity with the police is not Hitchcock's favorite mode of operation, to be sure; he is more likely to put himself in cahoots with a villain, as he does in, say, *Rope* and *Psycho*. But it is worth recalling that there are different kinds of police in his films. These include the utterly ineffectual cops who appear in early shots of *The Wrong Man* just as they showed up in *Blackmail, Shadow of a Doubt,* and *Rope,* always uniformed and useless; and there are the plainclothes cops that occasionally serve a purpose, such as the boyfriend in *Shadow of a Doubt* and the inspector in *Dial "M" for Murder.* The lieutenant in *The Wrong Man* stands between these extremes, doing his job methodically and with a great show of fair play that is, ironically, worthless. Hitchcock gives him much attention during the movie's first half, and partly identifies with him in the high-angle moment just cited, not because he admires the officer (he's fully aware that Bowers is dead wrong in everything he's doing to noncriminal Manny, and that his potency rests on social lies and institutional mistakes), but because he is a key instrument in one of the narrative's grand designs: to function as a contemporary Job story in which the filmmaker giveth and taketh away. For these tasks, Hitchcock has a pair of tools at his disposal – physically, the overwhelming mechanisms of modern criminal-justice procedure, centering on the lieutenant; and psychologically, the guilt-generated morality of the 1950s, embodied by poor Manny himself.

The Wrong Man is not Hitchcock's only Job story. Many of his films can be read in this light, if only in the sense that the narrative plunges a protagonist into chaos, then removes much (if not all) of the burden through some degree of conventional plot resolution. *The Wrong Man* stands as an exceptionally straightforward example of the breed, however, since (every)Manny is explicitly a Decent Person who is tested by ordeals involving the well-being of himself and his family. As elsewhere in Hitchcock's work, the wife seems more aware than the husband that overwhelmingly large forces are at work and that no ordinary human action can satisfactorily resolve all aspects of the situation. One thinks of Jo McKenna's philosophical "Que Sera, Sera" (in the 1956 version of *The Man Who Knew Too Much*) when one hears Rose's statements – even more fatalistic than Jo's song – that it doesn't matter what one does or where one is, since the powers of aggression will claim dominion whenever they wish to. These assertions are allegedly demented, yet they ultimately prove to be prescient, since it is by what appears to be a supernatural intervention – not a human act – that Manny's crisis is overcome.

Rose's assertions also balance certain elements in the narrative that tend to minimize some aspects of this crisis – that is, to engage in a denial of reality in quintessential 1950s style. One example is lawyer O'Connor's assurance that his fee "will take care of itself" once the case is over. A more general example is Hitchcock's decision not to point out (much less underline) the fact that Manny's financial troubles are multiplying even as he works his way out of the policemen's clutches: Not only O'Connor's fee, but bills from the psychiatrist and the sanitorium will have to be "taken care of" once the criminal-justice ordeal is over, and as far as we know Rose's teeth haven't been fixed yet. These considerations make the "happy" ending seem still more hollow and artificial.

This ending, with the Balestrero family seen in extreme long shot – living happily in Florida, according to a perfunctory printed statement – is itself an example of the film's reality-denying mechanism, one of its most 1950s-ish components. It is possible that Hitchcock allows the narrative this oddly indulgent dimension in order to mitigate the darkness and harshness that otherwise predominate, not wishing to alienate his mid–1950s audience by stressing unpleasant elements, which, moreover,

76

can be discovered without directorial prodding by any spectator willing to think about the story. It is more likely, however, that Hitchcock is engaging in a profoundly ironic maneuver by sardonically *mirroring* a shallow variety of midcentury optimism in the deep structure of his narrative. Some combination of both these practices can be seen as an animating factor in film noir (especially noir endings) generally. Their presence here solidifies the link between the noir cycle, which itself has frequent sadomasochistic overtones, and *The Wrong Man,* which comes closer than any other Hitchcock film – including such often-cited candidates as *Rope, Notorious,* and *Shadow of a Doubt* – to being a full-fledged noir. (*The Wrong Man* fails to satisfy some often-encountered qualifications for membership in the noir club, such as possession of a mazelike plot and a fragmented camera/editing style; but then, the qualifications for this club are notoriously ill defined.)

Examining the reality-denying aspect of *The Wrong Man* further, to what extent does this shut the characters out of the real world altogether? Rose does enter a fugue state of devastating severity, to the point where she is unable to communicate with Manny on even the simplest level. Manny never approaches such a condition, however, for at least two reasons:

1. As the "man of the house" in a patriarchal society, he is expected by his culture and himself to show more strength than his wife, even if this increases the pressures on him beyond the point where he can effectively cope with them. Manny's effort to counterbalance his wife's "weakness," signified by her breakdown, is successful at first but (along with the other burdens facing him) leads eventually to his own loss of traditional male potency, evidenced in two ways: his hand-wringing despair at O'Connor's announcement that the trial ordeal must start over from the beginning, and his abrupt recourse to supernatural help.
2. In a use of psychoanalytic theory that is characteristic of both Hitchcock and the noir tradition, the film inscribes Manny in the role of ego for his family and for the narrative. His children represent forces of the id, especially the youngest, who feels free to gorge himself on dad's lasagna and whine about his missed music lesson, even while the rest of the family is brooding over its crisis. Rose's psychodynamics are dominated by superego forces, which eventually overwhelm her with heavily masochistic guilt feelings as inescapable as they are irrational. Manny stands between these extremes, controlling his id impulses (he plays at wagering but rarely goes to the track) and to some extent his superego drives (although he behaves submissively for the police, he never tells them

what they'd like to hear) while serving, in the narrative itself, as a self-aware intermediary between wife/children and film/audience.

There is nothing very subtle or sophisticated about this kind of psychologizing, but its presence helps explain why Manny keeps his sanity in the film while his wife goes swiftly and almost irreparably mad. Embodying a sort of tense bourgeois rationality is one of his chief roles in Hitchcock's scheme, as important as his parallel role of embodying culturally determined guilt feelings. The fact that these roles are incompatible with any chance at happiness, and probably with each other, is one of the factors that make the film's texture so richly ambiguous. In any case, Manny's ability to keep a grip on his sanity does not prevent the film itself from engaging in conspicuous wish fulfillment by refusing to acknowledge the growing severity of Manny's problems and the unlikelihood of a happy ending in Florida or anywhere else.

It must further be asked whether the climax of the story – the concurrence of Manny's prayer with the capture of the "right" man – represents a further instance of reality denial and wish fulfillment, or whether it is intended as a "realistic" plot twist to be accepted literally. Those who believe in the swift efficacy of intercessory prayer will feel no ambivalence about this matter, while those who do not so believe will reject the resolution as insufficient and even nonsensical. Hitchcock grew up in a Roman Catholic tradition that surely shared many characteristics with the tradition represented by Manny's mother. However, there is no evidence that Hitchcock retained the beliefs of that tradition to a significant degree in his adult life – indeed, there is evidence to the contrary – and it is certainly true that no other Hitchcock film relies on such an overtly and specifically religious intervention for the resolution of a key narrative dilemma, or of any narrative dilemma at all. There are three possible explanations of why this happens in *The Wrong Man:*

1. The film adheres to Manny Balestrero's real-life experience. However, the facts appear to have been different from the way Hitchcock depicts them. Calling the dissolve from Manny's face to that of the criminal "a dramatic contrivance," Marshall Deutelbaum reports that while the real Balestrero "was a religious man and prayed at his trial," he was "not praying, but playing in the Stork Club band" at the time when the real criminal was arrested.[6] Hitchcock changed the actual events of the Balestrero case in many ways, treating it not as an inviolable set of facts, but rather as a vehicle for exploring themes that interested him.
2. This is an instance of Hitchcock submitting his will to that of his char-

acters; *they* believe Manny's prayer effected the resolution of his problem, and the film depicts the event accordingly. Again, however, if Hitchcock is willing to alter facts of the Balestrero case vis-à-vis what happened in real life, he would probably not hesitate to alter them vis-à-vis the attitudes of the on-screen characters. Their religious beliefs do not play a strong role during most of the narrative, moreover.

3. Hitchcock emphasizes Manny's prayer not because he respects the facts of the Balestrero case or the characters' feelings about those facts, but for the opposite reason: His interest piqued by Manny's religious nature, he has decided to explore his own ideas about the connection between spiritually oriented human activities and the material world in which such activities take place – especially in film, a materialistic medium (tied to photochemistry and mechanics) by its very nature. Never afraid to manipulate a narrative in whatever ways he sees fit, he unhesitatingly chooses to stress what would have otherwise been a fleeting and peripheral element of the movie.

This last explanation best fits *The Wrong Man* and its unusual climax. It also links the film to a tradition of spiritually inclined cinema that Paul Schrader has described as "transcendental" in style.[7] Hitchcock is not mentioned in Schrader's book on the subject, but a number of Hitchcock films follow the general pattern that Schrader identifies as characteristic of transcendental film. This pattern has three stages:

1. "The everyday: a meticulous representation of the dull, banal commonplaces of everyday living...."
2. "Disparity: an actual or potential disunity between man and his environment which culminates in a decisive action...."
3. "Stasis: a frozen view of life which does not resolve the disparity but transcends it."[8]

This is almost a blueprint for some of Hitchcock's greatest work. Considering only the films analyzed at length in this book, one thinks of the "dull, banal commonplaces" of washroom and restaurant in *Blackmail,* Santa Rosa life in *Shadow of a Doubt,* Scottie's boredom in *Vertigo,* the constricted world of office and motel in *Psycho,* Bodega Bay's slow-witted approach to life and love in *The Birds.* One recalls (referring to the same films) the "disunity" and "decisive action" of Alice's killing, young Charlie's confrontation of her uncle, Scottie's discovery of Judy's identity, Lila's discovery of Mrs. Bates, and the attic attack on Melanie. And one notes the "frozen view of life" that characterizes our last view of the paintings by

79

Alice and Crewe, the static conversation in front of Santa Rosa's church, Scottie gazing from the tower, Norman huddled in his cell, and Mitch's car edging down a roadway thronged with birds.

Other films provide different examples, and in some cases stronger ones. But none is more aligned with Schrader's three-part schema than *The Wrong Man*. Manny's everyday life is exquisitely banal, and Hitchcock could not be more meticulous in representing its quotidian dullness or the grinding monotony that creeps into police and courtroom procedures. With the decisive action of his prayer — at once an attempt to transcend his stifling everyday life *and* his ultimate act of prostration before a dominating power — Manny opens a gaping disunity between his yearning spirit and the commonplace environment that has been suffocating it; and Hitchcock responds with a heroically conspicuous decisive action of his own, the dissolve linking Manny's face with that of the thief about to seal his own fate with a final, hopelessly failed crime. The movie then approaches stasis through Manny's interview with his emotionally paralyzed wife, and achieves that stasis with the valedictory shot of the reunited Balestrero family — frozen in Florida, in a long shot at once static, artificial, and (by design) terminally unconvincing.

If it is true that Manny's prayer constitutes a decisive action, splitting open a hitherto mechanistic and materially determined narrative world, one can ascribe to Hitchcock a strong interest in the nature and potential power of prayer. He explores this on two levels: a psychological level, since Manny's decision to pray reveals important things about his state of mind, and a spiritual level, since the prayer doesn't just comfort Manny but instantly changes the course of his life and the film itself.

Hitchcock's attitude toward the prayer is complex, however, and cannot be neatly characterized as reverent or even credulous. For one thing, the prayer and its result do not spring entirely from some spontaneous upsurge of faith in Manny's mind: In a shot of Manny entering a store early in the film, a clearly seen cross design on the door indicates that religious motifs and attitudes are a part of the world extending far beyond his own impulses and his mother's old-country beliefs. For another, the incident may be read as wholly serendipitous, with the prayer a simple lapse into wish fulfillment and reality denial, the capture an unrelated coincidence. Also, the prayer scene is itself ambiguous: Is the criminal captured because Manny prays, or is Manny moved to pray at this moment because of an intuitive knowledge that the criminal is about to be captured?

Such intuition would be in line with, say, the bond shared by the Charlies in *Shadow of a Doubt* or the nonrational (but accurate) feelings that lead

Constance Petersen and Babs Milligan to trust what appear to be dangerous men in *Spellbound* and *Frenzy,* respectively. The existence of such intuitive force fields is felt more than once in Hitchcock's work, signifying his sense (crystallized most powerfully in *The Birds*) that heaven and earth may indeed contain more things than are dreamed of by a materialistic philosophy. He refuses to specify the nature of these things in any but tentative ways, however, such as *The Wrong Man*'s suggestion that they may occasionally take a form congruent (not necessarily identical) with that of traditional religious faith and a belief in the power of prayer; and that the closest Manny may come to transcendence of his passive/masochistic daily life is, ironically, through an ultimate act of submission to the ultimate dominating power. Beyond this, we – and Hitchcock's characters – are free to speculate.

Notes

1. Warren Susman, with the assistance of Edward Griffin, "Did Success Spoil the United States? Dual Representations in Postwar America," in *Recasting America: Culture and Politics in the Age of the Cold War,* ed. Lary May, Chicago: The University of Chicago Press, 1989, pp. 19–37, cited at 22.

2. Fred Camper, "*Shoah*'s Absence," *Motion Picture* 1:3, 1987, pp. 5–6, cited at 6.

3. Susan Sontag, *On Photography.* New York: Farrar, Straus & Giroux, 1977, pp. 14–15.

4. Robert Stam, *Subversive Pleasures: Bakhtin, Cultural Criticism, and Film.* Baltimore: Johns Hopkins University Press, 1989, p. 63. Hitchcock creates verbal/visual puns a number of times in his work. Stam also notes such examples as "bird's-eye view" in *Psycho* – he might have added *The Birds* – and the use of a crane shot to introduce Marion Crane.

5. It may be questioned whether a 1950s audience would have perceived its own era in this way and whether it would have responded to this level of the film; but a perceptive segment of the 1950s intelligensia was vocally aware of conformity and related attitudes as significant problems, and Hitchcock was capable of operating on levels not necessarily accessible to popular audiences on first viewings.

6. Marshall Deutelbaum, "Finding the Right Man in The Wrong Man," in *A Hitchcock Reader,* eds. Marshall Deutelbaum and Leland Poague. Ames: Iowa State University Press, 1986, pp. 207–18, cited at 210.

7. Paul Schrader, *Transcendental Style in Film: Ozu, Bresson, Dreyer.* Berkeley and Los Angeles: University of California Press, 1972.

8. Ibid., pp. 38–51.

5
Vertigo

The title could have been, *To Lay a Ghost.*
— *Vertigo* screenwriter Samuel Taylor

If there is one element that crystallizes the impact, ingenuity, and sheer strangeness of *Vertigo* (1958), it is the repeated shot representing Scottie/ James Stewart's troubled gaze into an abyss far below. Hitchcock achieved this effect of merciless disorientation by tracking away from the subject of the shot while simultaneously zooming toward it, thus combining two shooting devices with very different implications. Tracking involves a movement of the camera (and, by extension, the director and spectator) with relation to the shot's primary subject. Zooming, by contrast, allows the equivalent of such movement to appear on-screen with no actual camera motion (apart from the internal shifting of the lens mechanism) taking place.

The choice of tracking or zooming indicates a directorial decision about how the subject of the shot will appear, frame by frame, on the screen. The choice also indicates a decision as to how the camera (and the director and audience, for whom the camera is a surrogate) will relate to the subject. Tracking creates a physical change in the relative positions of camera and subject; zooming creates a heightening of attention and/or visual detail without movement. Reasons for the choice may be aesthetic, practical, or both.

By combining the track-out and zoom-in, Hitchcock devised a shot with few uses in standard film-narrative technique.[1] Its usefulness in *Vertigo*, however, is at least threefold. First, it provides a visual approximation of a psychological condition — extreme dizziness and disorientation — that is afflicting one of the film's protagonists, accomplishing this in a way that recalls (in its overt manipulation of reality) the German expressionism that influenced Hitchcock early in his career.[2] Second, it enhances audience identification with Scottie by providing information "through his eyes" both physically and psychologically, carrying to new heights the point-of-view approach that had already served Hitchcock well for many years. Third, it signifies ambiguous feelings of attraction–repulsion on Hitchcock's own part.

Hitchcock's work is often marked by a sense of mingled fascination and repugnance with regard to evil behavior, whether manifested by criminal action or by hatred, aggression, and chaos. This attraction–repulsion reaches its most explicit level in *Psycho*, with Marion's robbery/repentance and Norman's murder/cleanup. It is a characteristic of Hitchcock's cinema long before that film, however – recall Alice's ambivalent relationship with Crewe in *Blackmail*, for instance – and in *Vertigo* it finds a highly concentrated expression, particularly in the shot construction under discussion here, which allows the filmmaker to reach *toward* threatening spatial/visual terrain (via lens manipulation) while simultaneously reeling *away* from it (via camera movement).

Vertigo is a symphony of attraction–repulsion feelings projected by Hitchcock onto his characters: the feelings of Judy toward Scottie, who is both her victim and her loved one; the feelings of "Madeleine" (as impersonated by Judy) toward the grave; and most dramatically, those of Scottie toward Judy in the moments just before her death at the end of the film. Attraction–repulsion also marks the behavior of secondary and even minor characters: Midge, who evidently loves Scottie but has ended their engagement; Elster, who married the real Madeleine and now wishes her dead; even the coroner, who verbally damns Scottie without actually punishing him; and perhaps long-dead Carlotta, who gave up her child (albeit against her will) and then longed for its return.

In addition to its powerful expression of attraction–repulsion, *Vertigo* represents one of Hitchcock's deepest penetrations into two other dualities: authenticity–performance and reality–illusion. Both are evoked immediately in the opening title sequence, which mingles the authenticity and "reality" of live action with the artifice and illusion of animated imagery.

Beginning with the lower-left quarter of a woman's face, the shot underlying the credits then shifts to a close-up of the mouth, then moves up to reframe on the eyes – which reinforce their own lateral configuration (and prefigure the horizontal bar shape that will soon begin the story) by suddenly glancing left, right, straight. The shot then singles out the right eye, coming in for a more extreme closeup as the color changes from natural tints to a reddish hue.

The eye widens as the word *Vertigo* zooms slowly toward us out of the pupil. This image serves two functions. It prefigures various gestures toward subjects, including the zoom component of the track–zoom shot. And it evokes the notion of birth, connoting all kinds of creation – among them synthesis, fabrication, performance – and linking them intimately with the act of seeing. This motif continues with a spiral shape that approaches us from the eye's center, laying the groundwork for the film's hypnotic, vertiginous tone. The eye fades out as the spiral grows, to be followed by another spiral and then by other shapes, each giving birth to the next: starburst configurations, a sort of revolving nebula, an eyelike shape that does not revolve, two more spirals. A last spiral, turning counterclockwise, accompanies the reappearance of the eye (still drenched in red) and disappears into its depths just before Hitchcock's name appears from the same mysterious source.

The importance of dualities in *Vertigo* is reinforced by the initial images of the first two scenes after the credits. The opening chase sequence begins with a ladder rung dividing the screen horizontally, and the scene in Midge's apartment starts with Scottie's cane dividing the screen vertically.

The first of these moments is the bolder one, since the ladder-rung shot initially has an abstract appearance. Only after we've had sufficient time to wonder about its meaning do we see two hands come into view – whereupon the camera pulls back and we realize we have been viewing part of a ladder that figures in an action episode.

The switch from abstraction to figuration takes place in *time,* while the stark horizontality of the ladder rung divides the *space* of the screen. Duality and contrast of different kinds are thus established as major motifs of the film, and the sound track bears this out, with strange clanking sounds ringing out intermittently over Bernard Herrmann's swirling music. Other dualities of the scene involve costume (uniformed, nonuniformed police) and the surfaces on which the action takes place (flat = secure, sloping = dangerous).

But life–death soon becomes the dominant opposition – as Scottie makes the same jump that his colleague just completed, slides toward a chasm between roofs, and grabs a gutter that bends precariously under his weight. The cop turns back to help him, but not before Scottie looks down and sees the deadly drop beneath, which simultaneously approaches and recedes under his view. The cop calls, "Give me your hand," his voice muffled (to *our* ears) by Scottie's terror. As he reaches for Scottie, who is paralyzed by fear, he slips and falls to his death. Scottie watches him fall, twisting in the air, and sees his body lying on the pavement below. (Hitchcock gives the corpse a pinwheel configuration that painters and sculptors have used for centuries to convey a sense of dynamism without locomotion.) The scene fades out on Scottie's straining arms and downward-gazing face.

Another key thread of *Vertigo* is thus introduced: the idea of suspension, beginning with Scottie's literal suspension over the urban abyss. Scottie will soon be seen living in a state of suspension – in his work life, as a retired man with nothing much to do; and in his personal life, unable to commit himself to (or break away from) his former fiancée. Metaphorically, his position at the end of the first scene gives birth to this situation, which is another instance of Hitchcock transforming a verbal pun into a visual/narrative trope.

Scottie can also be seen as the heir to a slightly earlier Stewart character, L. B. Jefferies of *Rear Window*, who begins his story in a psychologically suspended state and ends it by dangling helplessly from a high place. Jefferies's condition is less drastic, however, since it is metaphorically linked with castration (his broken leg is a downward displacement of sexual anxiety and dysfunction), while Scottie's is related to an all-encompassing dread of decision, action, even life itself. Jefferies's situation is resolved, moreover, by an actual and visible fall, allowing his story to reach a satisfactory resolution, albeit an ironic and ambiguous one that (among other things) redoubles his disability. Within the action of *Vertigo*, Scottie *never* falls. His rescue remains implicit – and more mysterious than Jefferies's, which is aided by two policemen who cushion the impact of his (not very long) drop. Scottie's rescue is effected only by the filmmaker, if by anyone, and therefore comes under the same category as other "miraculous" events in Hitchcock's work, such as Uncle Charlie's escape from his pursuers and Manny Balestrero's deliverance. In all these cases, characters benefit from cinematic resources that are available only through Hitchcock's special attention.

As noted earlier, suspension in Hitchcock's films may be carried to the point of paralysis. One thinks of William Bendix's crippled character in *Lifeboat*, Montgomery Clift's morally immobile priest in *I Confess*, and of course the title character in *The Trouble with Harry*, the most immobilized (downright dead!) and yet the most mischievous of them all.

Scottie is the most sympathetic and the most extreme of such characters.

He begins the story by helplessly witnessing a death; later he is manipulated into a tragically similar situation when "Madeleine" meets her "death." While he is innocent of wrongdoing in both cases, there is something in him that leans away from satisfactory resolutions of hard situations – a fact borne out even in his relationship with Midge, which culminates when she reaches out desperately to him in the sanatorium, only to find that his inability to act has become all-consuming. Like the protagonist of John Barth's novel *The End of the Road*, he finds all movement so charged with awful possibilities that *no* movement seems the only recourse. Midge can only watch and wait, her own energetic personality infected with Scottie's spiritual malady.

Introducing another duality, the film's second scene crystallizes the split between Scottie and the kind of "normal, commonsense" person that Midge represents. In her apartment – with large windows showing a bright, airy San Francisco cityscape – she sits at a drawing table to the left, while right of center Scottie sits in an easy chair, balancing a cane on his right-hand fingertips. This balancing act has a playful air, starkly opposed to the rooftop scene we've just witnessed; yet the vertically held cane has several functions. It contrasts with (and "balances") the horizontal ladder rung that opened the story. It also divides the frame precisely in half, walling Scottie off from his companion. Indeed, it bisects the screen itself, establishing Scottie as subtly cut off, *divided* from much of the world in which he lives. Moreover, it symbolizes his precarious balance on a number of levels: physically, between disability and capability; psychologically, between lurking phobia and momentary confidence; emotionally, between fulfillment and boredom; romantically, between commitment and noncommitment.

In addition, the cane's precise division of the screen signals the presence of Hitchcock as the presiding influence over this shot – which, after the tumultuous introductory scene, is the first orderly, everyday-life shot of the film – and hence over the entire movie. The dressing-screen shot in *Blackmail* did something similar, demonstrating the director's ability to order, classify, and arrange his characters at will. Hitchcock's orderliness is a superego function, of course, and a zealous one at that: a place for everyone and everyone in his/her place. He seems at times to be straining overtly against the disorder/chaos/evil that itself strains (both overtly and covertly) to erupt in his narratives. He literally pigeonholes his characters in little hiding places: One thinks of Melanie's phone booth in *The Birds,* the record-store booth in *Strangers on a Train,* the fruit cellar in *Psycho* – and perhaps of Norman Bates's speech about "private traps," as well.

Midge's apartment has a comfortable look. Still, the first thing Scottie says (twice) is "Ouch," and when Midge questions his "aches and pains," he blames his soreness on a therapeutic corset that "binds" him. (One remembers the same actor squirming with itchy discomfort in a plaster cast at the beginning of *Rear Window*; both Scottie and Jefferies have been immobilized partly by the medical profession.) In a moment we see that Midge is sketching a brassiere, linking the characters by (of all things) a preoccupation with underwear. Scottie rejoices that his corset will come off tomorrow and that he'll be able to toss his cane "out the window," an ironic turn of phrase considering how he came to need it.

He and Midge then discuss his acrophobia: "What a moment to find out I had it!" he exclaims. It is clear that Scottie did not acquire this condition, and its symptom of vertigo, as a result of his traumatic experience during the rooftop chase; rather, that experience revealed the preexisting condition to him. This seemingly small distinction has large implications. A number of terms might serve as metaphors for Scottie's problem, from "fatal flaw" to "Achilles heel," and many of them relate in some way to the concept of original sin. Scottie's condition is indeed *original*, a part of his being and his nature, rather than an illness or eccentricity imposed on him by the random circumstances of an active life. It has been observed of Hitchcock's films, both disparagingly and sympathetically, that things happen *to* his characters – that they are more acted on than acting. There is truth to this, although it can hardly be called a "failing" in Hitchcock's worldview. In Scottie's case, however, he is specifically not acted on by his rooftop trauma. If he has been acted on at all, it is by fate, shaping the deepest characteristics of his personality before adulthood and perhaps before birth itself. And where we see fate at work in Hitchcockian cinema, we see the filmmaker at work, as well.

Similar observations may be made regarding other characters in *Vertigo*. For all the complexity of this film, the root causes of personality traits are rarely revealed to us or explored with any thoroughness – in contrast to the many clues we're given regarding, say, the disorders of Bruno Anthony and Norman Bates in their films. What drove Elster to concoct such a complicated and malign scheme? What, aside from infatuation with Elster – which she seems to have overcome easily enough in the second half of the movie – led Judy to carry off such an elaborate and sexually intimate masquerade? These mysteries relate to the off-screen lives of the characters, and while it may be true that "there's an answer for everything," as Scottie says in San Juan Bautista, the filmmaker is not generous in giving us the keys to their solutions.

Hitchcock further demonstrates his control over the characters and their destinies when Scottie decides to cure his vertigo by acclimatizing himself to heights, right there in Midge's living room. He climbs onto a footstool and then a larger stool, each time chanting, "I look up, I look down," until his eyes fall on the drop-off outside Midge's window,³ whereupon he faints into her arms. The faint is filmed in a significant way: Scottie falls gently into Midge's embrace, as he if were standing on the floor next to her, not elevated several feet in the air. In such "miraculous" moments, as we have seen, Hitchcock frequently reveals himself.

As if to confirm his presence here, Hitchcock makes his cameo appearance in the next shot, which shows the exterior of Elster's business establishment. The entrance recedes from the camera horizontally, contrasting with the vertical drop we have just seen. Elster proves to be a wealthy shipbuilder who misses the San Francisco of old, which he characterizes by listing four qualities: color, excitement, power, and freedom. (The last two items in that list will be mentioned again in the film, to devastating effect.) As he speaks, revealing that he knows about Scottie's recent troubles from newspaper reports, a large window (echoing the windows in Midge's home) gives a glimpse of the size and power of Elster's business. Scottie's back is to Elster, and us, as they talk, but the mood becomes more intense (the camera swooping *toward* Elster, then *away* from Scottie) as Elster draws Scottie into discussion of his wife and the danger she allegedly faces.

Hitchcock never lets us know Elster well enough to determine whether his scheme is the result of simple malignity or of a clinically deranged personality. His success in business (even if he did marry into the company he runs) might suggest that he is a strong and capable individual, if an evil one. One remembers that Hitchcock is often unflattering to the business world, however, and soon he gives a further clue to the possibly psychotic origins of Elster's machinations. Scottie expresses extreme, almost comical skepticism on hearing of Madeleine's supposed possession by Carlotta, and suggests medical attention for her. Elster says he wants more information about her activities "before committing her to *that* kind of care," subtly stigmatizing a "kind of care" that Hitchcock himself takes quite seriously in such films as *Spellbound* and *Marnie,* where psychoanalytic theory (with or without psychoanalysts) is central. Elster is playing a role here, of course. Yet his inflection also anticipates Norman Bates's angry reference to "some place," similarly referring to a mental hospital or asylum. This connection between Elster and Norman, however slight, may indicate Hitchcock's view of Elster's mental stability.

Elster insists he needs "a friend" to do this job, and Scottie doesn't protest the remark, even though he's hardly a "friend" of this long-unseen college acquaintance. Already wearing a look of worry and perplexity that prefigures his feelings much later in the film, Scottie agrees to "see" the woman that evening. The choice of verb is important, not only for the coming scene but for the profoundly visual and performance-oriented film as a whole.

Elster has been putting on an act for Scottie, to be sure. But the film assumes its full force as a study of performance and reality–illusion when Scottie first sees Madeleine (whose name has not been spoken yet) in a moment marked by eloquent camera movement and expressive cross-cutting between the two, rendered more complex by the exact positions of their faces from moment to moment. Both are seen largely in profile – that is, they are only half-seen, and (with one exception) we don't have *Psycho*'s persistent mirrors to provide secondary glimpses of their hidden halves. For any spectator not completely new to the film, Madeleine is obviously "performing" for Scottie in every sense of the term. This is a key moment, and Hitchcock presents it wordlessly, as he does the next scene, in which Scottie follows Madeleine to a florist's shop where she stands (in an important motif) surrounded by flowers. The most telling shot displays Scottie peering through a crack in a doorway, with Madeleine clearly framed in a mirror to the left – another split-screen effect that conveys Scottie's voyeurism, Madeleine's status as a performer and object for his gaze, and the filmmaker's explicit control over both of them.

The film's next portion continues to operate on a completely visual level with few spoken words, expressive of Scottie's growing fixation on Madeleine and the voyeurism through which this is manifested. They go to a graveyard, where she gazes at the tombstone of Carlotta Valdes, and to a museum, where she gazes at a portrait of Carlotta that features the same bouquet and the same swirling, vertiginous hairstyle that Madeleine has. Dialogue returns when Scottie questions a hotelkeeper about Madeleine's visits to a small rented room, only to discover that she has disappeared from a place where he saw her moments before. This disappearance is never explained, and signals yet again the filmmaker's ability and willingness to manipulate the realities of his story. (The scene is a ghostly parody of Scottie's miraculous transference from the danger of the rooftops to the safety of Midge's apartment; it also recalls Uncle Charlie's mysterious disappearances in *Shadow of a Doubt*.)

Midge guides Scottie to a bookstore where a local-history expert tells how Carlotta's life was ruined by the machinations of a man whose "power and . . . freedom" enabled him to keep their child while abandoning her to loneliness, madness, and suicide. Elster fleshes out the story more during Scottie's next visit, insisting that Madeleine is "no longer [his] wife" but is possessed by Carlotta, her dead great-grandmother, during her wandering spells. Scottie trails her again, and the next climactic moment arrives when she wanders to a spot near the Golden Gate Bridge, pensively throws blossoms from her Carlotta-style bouquet into the water, and then leaps off the bank. Scottie rescues her, carries her limp body to his car, and speaks her name for the first time. Next we find Scottie stoking the fire and having a drink in his living room. Madeleine's clothes are hung up to dry in his kitchen, and she (presumably nude) is unconscious in his bed, mumbling the mad Carlotta's ritual lament: "Have you seen my child?"

Vertigo has taken a straight trajectory toward this moment of meeting; every element of the story has played a part in bringing it about. Scottie is discreet and chivalrous when Madeleine awakes, but her spell over him is evident in his every gesture, and in the haunting music that wafts through the sound track. Framed in the doorway, she makes a seductive entrance, posing as carefully as when she first appeared before Scottie in the restaurant. In both scenes, however, Scottie also plays an assumed role. In the restaurant he played a disinterested spectator, pretending to have no interest in the woman he came specifically to see. (Hitchcock makes canny use of spectator–performer ambiguity more than once in his films; in *Rope*, for instance, the ghoulish "performers" and invited "audience" function as visual objects and subjects for each other.) Now, in more intimate circumstances, Scottie again hides essential aspects of his identity and purpose – grilling Madeleine, like the detective he is, but concealing his profession and his relationship with her husband. When she asks what he does for a living, he uses the codewords for her own trancelike activity: "Wander about."

The performances here are impressive on the movie-acting level as well as the narrative level. Stewart expertly conveys Scottie's mixture of compassion for Madeleine, bewitchment with the mystery surrounding her, and absorption in his own growing infatuation. Novak is also in top form, especially given the complexity of this moment for her character. For spectators new to the film, Madeleine must seem an alluring woman of mystery; for those who have seen it before, she must appear an equally alluring actress falling under the spell of both her own role and the one-man audience for whom she is playing it. All these elements converge in a romantically and sexually charged moment when Scottie's hand touches Madeleine as she reaches for a coffee cup, often a Hitchcockian symbol for mingled civility and fragility. Elster then calls, and before Scottie can leave the telephone Madeleine has gathered her clothes and gone – observed by Midge (in her car), who delivers a brief and bitter soliloquy: "Well now, Johnnie-o, was it a ghost? Was it fun?"

Height continues to figure in the narrative's developments. Madeleine says Coit Tower was the landmark that guided her to Scottie's home for her next encounter with him. More important is their visit to a sequoia forest – one of the eeriest scenes in Hitchcock's work, with moody poetics that seem all the more vivid since the episode does little to advance the plot or provide specific new knowledge about the characters. They marvel at the age of the tall trees: "Some 2,000 years or more," Scottie says, to which Madeleine replies, "The oldest living things." We see them in long shot and hear their voices at a distance (the sustained chords on the sound track recall Herrmann's score for the dark first sequence of *Citizen Kane*) until Madeleine says the trees remind her of her own death.

After a close-up we return to long shot, then to medium shot as they approach a cross section of a cut-down tree. Events in human history are noted along the concentric circles of the trunk, which recall Dante's circles of hell as well as Scottie's condition of vertigo. Madeleine traces the times of her own birth and "death" with a black-gloved hand. Apparently in a semitrance, she wanders away from Scottie, who catches up with her and interrogates her about her spells. She begs him to take her "somewhere in the light," and (in one of the film's many dissolves) the scene moves to the seashore. Scottie tells Madeleine he is "responsible" for her since he saved her life, and at this point there is a subtle and disorienting spatial shift. Scottie and Madeleine appear to face each other directly when seen from the side; yet one shot in the sequence places Madeleine at an odd angle to Scottie and to the camera, heightening the sense of otherworldliness already stressed by haunting music and the subdued tones of the performers.

Hugging a scraggly seaside tree, Madeleine likens her life to "walking down a long corridor that . . . that once was mirrored, and fragments of that mirror still hang there. And when I come to the end of the corridor, there . . . there's nothing but darkness. And I know that when I walk into the darkness, that I'll die." She has never come to the corridor's end, she adds – except once, when she jumped into the bay. It is significant that this speech sounds like the description of a dream but refers to her waking life, or to a profound hallucination that mingles freely with it.

Scottie questions her further, and she remembers looking into a freshly dug grave that was somehow meant for her. Scottie fishes for more facts that would give him a "key" to the mystery, and Madeleine suggests that madness could be the explanation. Running from him to the waterside, she insists that she is possessed, and they kiss as the sea heaves melodramatically behind them. Fade to black, on an image that illustrates Hitchcock's tendency to punctuate a film's most emotionally meaningful moments with touches of brazen romanticism and theatricality that recall pulp-fiction conventions. By undercutting whatever "realism" he has striven for thus far, he intensifies the otherworldliness that is the film's most insinuating quality.

Concern with artifice carries into the next scene, which fades in on Midge painting in her apartment. Unable to elicit more communication from Scottie than a vague statement about "wandering . . . round and about," she announces that she has returned to her "first love," a phrase that could refer to Scottie himself but instead means making art. Framed in profile, as Madeleine has often been, she offers to display her work: Carlotta Valdes's portrait with her own face superimposed on it. Depressed and angry, Scottie leaves while Midge defaces the picture and hurls her brush at the picture window, tacitly recalling Scottie's acrophobia and his whimsical description of how he would rid himself of his cane.

Scottie wanders through the night, returns home, and receives a visit from Madeleine, whose dream has recurred. He completes her description of it, identifying the setting as the San Juan Bautista mission. Insisting that a visit there will dispel the dream's power, he takes her (in an overhead shot) to the door, which fills the screen in an example of what William Rothman calls Hitchcock's "white-flash" moments.[4] Then the two are seen driving to San Juan Bautista – her face covered with enigmatic emotions, the interpretation of which depends on whether one has seen the film before.

In the livery stable of the mission, Scottie gives Madeleine a dose of reality therapy – insisting that she has been there before – but she maintains that her previous visit was in a time far earlier than he has in mind. In an exultant orgy of rationality and positivism, he points out details that root her dream in the here-and-now rather than a mystical past. "Try for me," he exhorts, gazing at her profile although we see her full face. "No one possesses you," he soon adds, even as *he* tries to possess her with his arms and his powerful feelings. She breaks away and heads for the tower, saying, "It wasn't supposed to happen this way." The scene ends with her apparent fall and with Scottie standing in shock before heading down the stairs, filmed from above so that the depth of the stairwell fills the screen (Fig. 8). A final shot of the tower gives it phallic prominence, ironically stressing Scottie's impotence.

The remaining portion of *Vertigo* is unusual for its depiction of a severely and conspicuously neurotic hero, not an everyday feature of mainstream cinema in this period. His disturbance becomes full blown in a dream sequence, which, unlike Madeleine's presumably imaginary nightmare, we are shown. Its most important details are an animation – the most deliberately artificial type of cinematic image – of a pulsating and exploding bouquet; the image of Scottie's vanishing and reappearing face, framed by lines re-

Figure 8. Attraction–repulsion: Scottie (James Stewart) confronts his worst fears in *Vertigo*. (Museum of Modern Art/Film Stills Archive. Copyright © by Universal City Studios, Inc. Courtesy of MCA Publishing Rights, a division of MCA, Inc.)

ceding toward a vanishing point; and the silhouette of his body falling toward the mission's roof. In the latter image, Scottie's arms are bowed – harking back to the pinwheeled shape of the sprawled policeman in the first scene and prefiguring Scottie's own posture in the last moment of the film.

From his terrified face we dissolve to the exterior of a sanitorium where Scottie is confined. Although it is hardly the horrific place that Norman envisages in *Psycho,* with "cruel eyes studying you" and other awful features, it is not more comforting or effectual than the institution that holds Rose in *The Wrong Man.* Its irrelevancies include a Mozart recording that Midge plays for Scottie, calling it "the broom that sweeps the cobwebs away." Scottie glances in her direction but never speaks, sitting corpselike and unresponsive. He is now the possessed figure of the film, his precarious psychological balance tilted drastically toward mute paralysis. "John-o, you don't even know I'm here, do you?" asks Midge.

The diagnosis is "acute melancholia, together with a guilt complex," according to the doctor, who also says the prognosis "could depend" on Scottie himself. This resting of future health on the patient's own shoulders must be considered a designation of "responsibility," a concept that was stressed by the coroner during the disastrous inquest. (Scottie himself also used this word to describe his relationship with Madeleine during their seaside conversation.) Hitchcock evidently intends the spectator to side strongly with Scottie against the coroner's indirect, yet scathing condemnation; still, some ambiguity may be sensed in the filmmaker's attitude toward Scottie at this point. Scottie's vertigo is an "original" condition that has been settled on him since birth, and it is this condition that impeded him in preventing Madeleine's apparent death. Yet he was complicitous in the events leading to this apparent death – falling in love with, and assuming responsibility for, a married woman who necessarily conducted most of her life (in its normal and abnormal aspects) away from his presence and influence.

Nor has death decreased his passion: Midge states that he loved Madeleine and still does. Midge then leaves the movie, walking forlornly down one of Hitchcock's gloomiest corridor-tunnels. Yet there is light at the end of it, literally, hinting that her future might not be altogether bleak now that Scottie is out of it. Just before the fade reaches black, she stops her movement – instead of continuing out of the corridor – and stands before the window as if meditating. This could be an accident of editing, with the shot allowed to continue an instant after the actress stopped acting; it can also be seen as a subtly expressive moment, with Midge hesitating one last moment before completely leaving Scottie's life. (It also anticipates the end of *Marnie,*

Figure 9. Reflections of Madeleine: Judy (Kim Novak) found by Scottie (James Stewart) in *Vertigo*. (Museum of Modern Art/Film Stills Archive. Copyright © by Universal City Studios, Inc. Courtesy of MCA Publishing Rights, a division of MCA, Inc.)

when the car containing Mark and Marnie "does not quite complete its action before The End," as Warren Sonbert has noted.[5])

The film's next portion begins formally, with a pan across the city; large dark areas among the buildings evoke the darkness now at Scottie's heart. We find him outside Madeleine's building, where a one-way traffic sign (signaling his heightened obsessiveness) is prominently framed along with a car like Madeleine's. This is the first of several doppelgängers he will encounter – including Madeleine look-alikes in Ernie's restaurant and in the museum with Carlotta's portrait, and finally Judy outside a florist's shop.

Their first conversation (in a hotel, home of transients and outsiders) is framed in close-up and dramatic two-shot, with Scottie at once menacing and pathetic in his stance across the room from her (Fig. 9). She calls herself "just a girl," showing documents in her wallet to prove her identity. Hitchcockian women frequently have insecure senses of their own identities, with varying consequences: One thinks of Alice in *Blackmail* feeling threatened by a sign ("White for Purity") bearing her last name, of young Charlie feeling bound to her older male namesake, of the shifting names and identities asserted by Marion Crane and Marnie Edgar, and, for contrast, of the dazzling impression made by Lisa Carol Freemont proudly proclaiming her selfhood in *Rear Window*, complete with dramatic pauses and lighting effects. Judy's weak and defensive stance has double significance, reflecting what probably is a deprecatory self-image (a result of patriarchal forces both external and internalized) and also the need to project a personality very different from Madeleine's glamorous and seductive presence.[6] It may kindle a spark of sympathy for Judy, however, even in a spectator who knows the movie's course.

Scottie leaves and Judy remains in the frame with the back of her head to us, then turns into profile and continues turning until she gazes directly toward (although not *into*) the camera. The background dims and the shot dissolves to the church tower, leading to a flashback of (the true) Madeleine's death and then to Judy's voice-over narration – as she writes to Scottie, the camera slowly circling from profile to frontal view – of the truth about Elster's murder scheme and her own love for Scottie. She tears the letter up and throws it away; other Hitchcock women, including Marion Crane and Melanie Daniels in later films, make a similar gesture.

Scottie and Judy spar in Ernie's restaurant, her apartment, and other places. Before long he begins his project of remaking her, in a clothing store where he insists on choosing every item. "I know the kind of suit that would look well on you," he says, the most reasonable man in the world. Judy rebels and Scottie, holding her so their images are doubled in a mirror, treats her exactly as a cajoling and badgering father might treat a reluctant child. Talk about patriarchy.

Back in her apartment, he admits he has no idea why he's manipulating her so, and when she finally agrees to wear the clothes he has selected, his eyes widen as he realizes her hair color must also be changed. She says she'll obey his wishes if he'll love her. The scene changes from her fireside to a hair salon, where white gowns and a clinical atmosphere recall Scottie's sanitorium. (Close-ups of Judy's face, hair, and hands recall the film's title sequence, as well.) Scottie prowls the apartment waiting for her, then insists that she pin her hair the way Madeleine did. She hesitates before entering the bathroom, always a significant location in Hitchcock's work. Scottie waits by the green-tinged window, then faces the green-tinged bathroom door; music croons in anticipation during the entire sequence. As she returns we see the back of his head, then his profile, and finally his full face as he turns toward her and the camera – and she isn't entirely real, bathed like a ghost in ghostly green light.

These are key moments in *Vertigo,* and in Hitchcock's history as a metteur-en-scène of his own controlling presence. Ever since he emerged from the sanitorium, Scottie has taken on the persona – without realizing it himself, at first – of a Pygmalion, a creator (or at least a molder) of human flesh, personality, and possibility. More specifically, he has become a director or a filmmaker, hunting for the proper "actress" to "cast" in the "production" that he has unconsciously conceived. On finding her, he naturally arranges for her costume and her makeup. The one detail that eludes him (he is new at this, after all) is her hairstyle, and this omission leads to a superbly expressive moment. She makes her entrance, Scottie realizes the imperfection, and then, as Fred Camper has perceptively observed, he requires a *retake* of the "shot," after she has perfected her appearance in the dressing room.

Judy loses her pallor as she advances, and as she kisses Scottie the camera revolves around them. The background also revolves, changing to black and then to the San Juan Bautista stable – a cinematic event that Scottie is somehow aware of, as discussed in Chapter 1. (The music underlines his sense of the occasion's weirdness, drastically changing its tone to that of a vaguely circuslike waltz.) The apartment swings back into view, and the shot ends with the lovers before the greenish pallor of the window.

"Where should we go for dinner?" is the pointedly quotidian question that opens the next scene, indicating that a catharsis (and/or orgasm) has taken place and that everyone is now relaxed. They agree on Ernie's, and amid chatter about how hungry she is – for what? one might ask – Judy asks Scottie to clasp the fatal necklace. He doesn't notice it when he looks at her directly, but rather when he sees her in the mirror. In a supremely Hitchcockian gambit, revealing both the state of Scottie's consciousness and the filmmaker's controlling presence, the camera moves to a closeup of Scottie's profile, then to the necklace. It then cuts to the appropriate detail of Carlotta's portrait, pulling away to reveal Madeleine gazing at it in a momentary flashback, and then back to the present, where Judy asks Scottie to "muss [her] a little" – something he will soon be vigorously doing.

The mission tower looks as potent as ever when they arrive there. Scottie tells Judy he needs her "to be Madeleine for a while," and that both of them will then "be free." Speaking of his last moments with Madeleine, he forces her into the church, where earlier he had chased her. The music returns to its antic waltz as he follows her up the lower stairs. The lengthening tunnel of the stairwell menaces him, but they both continue. She admits everything as he questions and brutalizes her; he only stops for a moment to gloat that he has "made it" up the stairs. A famous and harrowing shot reveals her feet limp on the stairs as Scottie drags her up. (The shot is analogous to that of Arbogast's feet in *Psycho*.) Using the key words "freedom" and "power," he deduces Judy's relationship with Elster, but loses his gloating strength as he chides her for being "sentimental" enough to keep Carlotta's necklace – and then recalls how much he loved her, calling her Maddy for the first time. She asserts that she endangered herself, by getting involved with him after the killing, only because she loved him so much.

They embrace, clearly renewing their love. It is here that the film's attraction–repulsion theme culminates, as Scottie grapples with simultaneous love and hatred for the woman who has changed his life forever. Then a dark figure suddenly appears. Judy says, "No." The figure says, "I hear voices." Scottie turns toward the figure, who steps forward to reveal herself as a nun. Judy shrieks and falls (unseen) from the tower. The nun speaks the last words of the film – "God have mercy" – and begins to pull the bell rope. The camera takes a midair position (eliminating the nun from view) as Scottie walks to the ledge and stands looking down, his arms slightly away from his body. The church bells compete with Herrmann's music as the scene fades to black.

We may see the nun as an arbitrary visitor to the plot; as an apparition comparable to the one Hitchcock saw in his early childhood, as discussed in Chapter 1; or – in the spirit of *The Wrong Man,* if we accept that film's climax on its most literal level – as a manifest sign that God is indeed having mercy on Scottie, if not on the woman he apparently still loves. In any case, Scottie's conquering of vertigo may be taken as a signal that his drastic act of self-therapy has worked. Noting that vertigo has a long history of association with insanity, Michel Foucault states that it "affords the delirious affirmation that the world is really 'turning around,'" such delirium being "a necessary and sufficient reason for a disease to be called madness."[7] Scottie's madnesses are over now; but his final pose suggests that his deepest sorrows may be just beginning.

Notes

1. Standard narrative shot styles, and the apparatus that implements them, are rooted in image-making conventions that may be called "artificially stabilized," in comparison with the instability of actual eye movements or with the nonstabilized style of some avant-gardists such as Stan Brakhage.

2. Hitchcock conceived the track–zoom effect in his min[...]
out to achieve it. He told Truffaut that when Joan Fon[...]
the inquest in *Rebecca* (1940), he "wanted to show how [...]
was moving far away from her before she toppled over," a se[...]
had once felt when he "got terribly drunk and . . . had the sensa[...]
was going far away." His technicians were not capable of reali[...]
Rebecca, he added: "The viewpoint must be fixed, you see, while th[...]
changed as it stretches lengthwise. I thought about the problem for fift[...]
the time we got to *Vertigo*, we solved it by using the dolly and zoom simult[...]
(François Truffaut, with the collaboration of Helen G. Scott, *Hitchcock*. Ne[...]
Simon & Schuster, 1984, p. 246.)

3. Robin Wood maintains that the point-of-view shot depicts not the drop-off outs[...]
Midge's window but the alleyway over which Scottie dangled in the first scene. Th[...]
evidence seems to me ambiguous. (Robin Wood, *Hitchcock's Films Revisited*. New
York: Columbia University Press, 1989, pp. 112, 235.)

4. William Rothman, *Hitchcock – The Murderous Gaze*. Cambridge, Mass.: Harvard University Press, 1982.

5. Warren Sonbert, "Hitchcock's *Marnie*." Personal communication, 1985.

6. Cf. Uncle Charlie as a personality projector in *Shadow of a Doubt*, and the
cultural-historical implications of this.

7. Michel Foucault, *Madness and Civilization: A History of Insanity in the Age of
Reason*, trans. Richard Howard. New York: Vintage, 1973, p. 100.

d's eye long before he figured
aine's character fainted at
she felt that everything
sation that he himself
ion that everything
ing this idea for
e perspective is
en years. By
neously."
y York:
de

ho

I'm like a one-eyed cat,
Peepin' in a sea-food store.
　　　　– Big Joe Turner, "Shake, Rattle & Roll"

"A blot on an honorable career" is how *New York Times* critic Bosley Crowther greeted the arrival of *Psycho* in 1960. By year's end the same pundit had rethought his position enough to include the film on his ten-best list, but controversy raged on elsewhere: Andrew Sarris placed it "in the same creative rank as the great European films," while Dwight Mac-donald called it "a reflection of a most unpleasant mind"[1] (Fig. 10).

Hitchcock may have felt a twinge on reading the negative assessments, since he had decided (as long ago as his *Blackmail* days) that reviewers should be taken seriously – not for the intelligence of their ideas, necessarily, but for their impact on the box office. On the latter score he needn't have worried: Audiences flocked to the movie from its first day, and haven't tired of it since.

Psycho is such a complex movie that many chapters could be (and have been) written on it, from any number of perspectives. I will begin this overview by concentrating on an area that has been undervalued (perhaps revealingly) in most of the literature: the film's preoccupation with anal-compulsive behavior, which recurs throughout the narrative in thinly disguised form, creating one of the richest "shadow film" structures in Hitchcock's oeuvre.

Psychoanalytic ideas must play a strong part in such an examination; while such theory has often been vulgarized in the course of film criticism, the appropriateness of certain Freudian notions to *Psycho* seems remarkably

Figure 10. A most unpleasant mind?: Norman (Anthony Perkins) and director (Alfred Hitchcock) prepare for a shot of *Psycho*. (Museum of Modern Art/ Film Stills Archive. Copyright © by Universal City Studios, Inc. Courtesy of MCA Publishing Rights, a division of MCA, Inc.)

strong. Norman's voyeurism and murderousness, for instance, are clarified by Freud's statement that in obsessional neurosis,

> regression of the libido to the antecedent stage of the sadistic-anal organization is the most conspicuous factor and determines the form taken by the symptoms. The impulse to love must then mask itself under the sadistic impulse. The obsessive thought, "I should like to murder you," means . . . nothing else but "I should like to enjoy love of you."[2]

Norman's confusions about sexual difference and appropriate sexual be- havior are similarly clarified by Freud's assertion that during the "pre- genital" phase (to which Norman has regressed) the

> contrast between *masculine* and *feminine* plays no part as yet; instead of it there is the contrast between *active* and *passive*. . . . That which

in this period seems masculine to us, regarded from the stand-point of the genital phase, proves to be the expression of an impulse to mastery, which easily passes over into cruelty. Impulses with a passive aim are connected with the erotogenic zone of the rectal orifice, at this period very important; the impulses of skoptophilia (gazing) and curiosity are powerfully active.[3]

It would be difficult to describe Norman with more chilling accuracy.

The first thing we see in *Psycho,* once the camera has passed through the hotel window and our eyes have penetrated the murky dimness, is a bathroom. Its white sink gleams faintly in the background as the camera searches for Marion Crane/Janet Leigh and Sam Loomis/John Gavin in the foreground. (A little later, Marion's own bathroom will be visible as she prepares to leave Phoenix with the stolen money.)

One of the next things we see is food: the lunch that Marion has been too occupied to eat and about which Sam speaks the first line of dialogue. Other objects in the room are equally commonplace but foreshadow later themes and events – especially the electric fan slashing the air with its blades. Sam crosses the room to stand in front of it, just as he mentions the grave of his debt-ridden father.

After one's first encounter with the film, such details take on a significance they could not have held initially. The same goes for dialogue in this scene, much of which reflects the film's interest in food and excess: Sam mentions Marion's lunch; she imagines cooking "a big steak" when they are married; she says she would "lick the stamps" for his alimony payments and that her long lunch hours give her boss "excess acid." As she dresses, an empty vase stands on a table behind her, splitting the frame – as other objects will do later – and prefiguring other receptacles, from a safe-deposit box to a toilet, that will affect her life.

Eating is the first step in the alimentary process that ends with defecation; the film's early food references are a kind of foreplay, drawing us toward a realm of anal anxiety where much of the movie will take place.[4] The hotel room is a location geared to genital activity – although in the case of Marion and Sam, not of a very fulfilling kind. As soon as we leave it, we head straight into an atmosphere of acutely arrested development. Not for the first time, Hitchcock signals the entry into a new narrative dimension with his personal appearance, standing outside the real-estate office where Marion works. We see him through a window, in keeping with the film's theme of voyeurism; he is facing away from the window, however, indicating that his control over the film's content precludes a need to observe it directly.

The next man we encounter, with a cowboy hat and build similar to Hitchcock's, is Cassidy, the real-estate customer. Although we don't see it right away, he has with him an object that is at once entirely commonplace and outrageously out of place: a packet of bills totaling far too much ($40,000) for any sensible businessperson to feel comfortable carrying around.

The symbolic nature of this object becomes apparent as we watch Cassidy's behavior. He is childish in his boasting about wealth, happiness, and success. He is domineering in his insistence that the business transaction be done according to his whims, and in his treatment not only of the women but of Lowery the boss, whom he humiliates (with his "bottle in the desk" remark) and then bullies into a drinking session. He is demanding of attention from everyone in the office. In all, he is an overgrown child who has not mastered — or cared to master — the rules of middle-class social intercourse.

Just as clear is the particular stage of childhood development in which he's stuck: the anal-sadistic phase. His packet of cash is a packet of excrement — which he has "made," of which he is proud, and with which he has no desire to part, at least before a proper and admiring fuss has been made over it by the women (Marion and Caroline) and the rather lame authority figure (Lowery) who are his audience.

Cassidy's conversation has as many biological overtones as that of Marion and Sam in their hotel room. He calls the weather "hot as fresh milk" and suggests that Lowery should "air-condition" not his office but (his syntax is significant) his employees. After embarrassing Lowery by revealing the presence of a liquor bottle in his desk, he responds to his own joke with a smarmy giggle, which he mockingly exaggerates by hiding his mouth with his hand — a gesture that Norman will echo in the aftermath of the shower scene.

Everyone reacts with a shocked look when he makes the decidedly improper gesture of waving his $40,000 under everyone's nose; it is obvious that such an object cannot decently be handled so openly or casually, especially when so *much* of it is present. The sense of money as filth, and money/filth as extremely threatening, is almost palpable. Lowery says it is "irregular" to make such a large transaction in cash, and Cassidy replies (in another double entendre) that it's his "private" money. Lowery does not want Cassidy's improper object in his office a moment longer than necessary — his discomfort, and that of his employees, is very plain — and orders Marion to deposit it immediately in a safe-deposit box, a proper receptacle where it will be safely out of sight. (Lowery has experience with secreting away forbidden stuff, e.g., the liquor in his desk drawer.) Marion and Caroline, not immune to naughty fascination, handle the money briefly before Marion puts it into an envelope (wrapping it hygienically in paper) and then into her purse.

This object, forbidden less because of its nature than because of the way it is retained and handled, will be the focus of the film's developments for quite a while. The next person to exhibit a compulsive retention syndrome is, of course, Marion herself. She does not deposit the money/excrement as instructed, but carries it home and puts it on her bed, the very place where she told Lowery she planned to spend the weekend. This shameful (disgusting!) act may remind us of Uncle Charlie in *Shadow of a Doubt,* whose excessiveness and lack of control are also symbolized by money – not placed in a proper location, but spilling unnoticed off his table and onto the floor. Later in *Shadow of a Doubt,* the same character articulates the Hitchcockian view of money in its most negative aspects. Questioning whether the "merry widows" he has murdered were truly "alive" or "human" at all, he portrays such women as parasites on the earnings of their dead husbands: "... drinking the money, eating the money... smelling of money." The connection of money with eating and stinking is queasily appropriate to Norman's case, and to some of the most fundamental twists in Hitchcock's dour worldview.

The camera looks at the money more than once, following Marion's gaze, as she packs for a journey. Although she has been restless throughout the scene, she sits on the bed – an image that hints at defecation – before placing the money in her purse. (Hitchcock's attachment of biological symbolism to purses has its plainest manifestation in *Marnie,* especially in its labial first shot.) She then picks up her suitcase and leaves, once again passing before her open bathroom door, the shower head particularly noticeable.

The anxiety generated by mishandled money/feces is even stronger now than in Lowery's office, in part because Marion not only is retaining the highly charged material on/in her person, but is transporting it very far from its proper repository. Discomfort is great for both parties when Lowery sees her as she heads out of town: She is sitting in her car, not where she ought to be sitting while disposing of such stuff.

Unreal voices assail her as she drives from Phoenix toward Fairvale, indicating Hitchcock-the-trickster's characteristic willingness to torment a character (even to think for her) and suggesting that Marion may have a touch of Norman in her psyche. Cassidy figures prominently in her interior mono-

Figure 11. The forbidden object: Rich and strange, Marion (Janet Leigh) enters a lavatory to handle her illicit money in *Psycho*. (Museum of Modern Art/ Film Stills Archive. Copyright © by Universal City Studios, Inc. Courtesy of MCA Publishing Rights, a division of MCA, Inc.)

logue – as biologically vulgar as ever, saying "kiss off" and "I'll replace [the money] with her fine soft flesh." He also says, "She sat there while I dumped it out," a sentence that makes the money = shit equation almost explicit.

Marion wears a faint, sardonic smile during some of this, but her reaction is one of extreme discomfort when a policeman interrogates her, after finding that she has engaged in another biological function (sleep) in an inappropriate place. She must fish her way past the money, hiding it between her body and the automobile seat, to grasp documents required by the cop. At the used-car dealership, she exchanges her dark-toned car for a model with a lighter color. (It's less resonant of excrement; the transaction is a mirror image of her earlier change from white to black underwear.) Before paying, she enters the lavatory to handle, examine, and break apart her forbidden horde (Fig. 11).

If there is any doubt regarding Hitchcock's scatalogical turn of mind throughout Marion's ordeal, a closeup of her first car's license plate lays it to rest: It is ANL-709, the letters spelling a revealing word while the numbers cushion an anuslike zero between two more substantial digits.

Although the ANL is the more blatant signifier here, the zero is also worth considering. Empty circles play a quiet, but important role in Hitchcock's films, the most celebrated example being Roger O. Thornhill's middle initial in *North by Northwest* – a letter that stands, he cheerfully reveals, for "nothing." He also acknowledges that it makes "rot" his "trademark," but he does not go on to admit the emptiness it symbolizes at the center of his life.

Other names, of characters and films, signal the pervasiveness of such emptiness in Hitchcock's world. His greatest achievements from this period – *Psycho, Vertigo, Rear Window* – have titles ending in O or its sound, acknowledging their vertiginously chaotic overtones. Midge, the friend who knows Scottie best in *Vertigo,* calls him John-o and Johnnie-o. Two people pronounce the name of *Psycho*'s doomed detective with a clipped Arb-O-gast inflection, and the movie's first protagonist is Marion rather than Marian. The fascination with O also relates to menacing circles in films from *Strangers on a Train* (record store, berserk merry-go-round) to *The Birds* (empty eye sockets, gaping mouths) and, perhaps most prominently of all, to *Psycho* – which culminates in its own empty sockets, and contains otherwise unexplained mysteries such as the *Er-O-ica* Symphony on Norman's phonograph. (The title, one letter short of "erotica," is spelled out near the center-hole of a circular disk with a circular label on a circular turntable.)

The empty circles take on still more meaning if one relates them metaphorically to eye sockets (some *are* eye sockets, as with Norman's mother and the farmer in *The Birds*) and thence to Margaret M. Horwitz's statement that "loss of sight is a customary figure for castration," an assertion she connects (via Stephen Heath) with Freud's discovery of the "substitutive relation between the eye and the male organ . . . in dreams and myths and phantasies." Bringing in the correlation between "vision and *power,*" Horwitz adds, "We can understand using blindness as a figure of castration for both males and females."[5] This concept is especially relevant to *Psycho*.

Marion disposes of her ANL–709 at the used-car dealership, and the rainstorm that comes down on her near the Bates Motel has a flushing and cleansing function. But her sin is already too great for such abstract absolution. Tormentingly, her vision is obscured (as it will be later by the shower curtain and shower water), and windshield wipers slash across the frame.

These hark back to the hotel room's spinning fan and anticipate the film's ultimate obscuring agent: Norman's murderous knife.

At the motel, Norman greets her with the words "Dirty night." But when he shows her Cabin No. 1, his banter dries up: Although he floods the bathroom with harsh light, he can't bring himself to say the word "bathroom," and she must utter the forbidden syllables for him.

She clutches her illicit purse-bundle as he invites her to share a sandwich with him. (She has mentioned that she needs some food, and well she might; we haven't seen her eat since she skipped lunch at the hotel room.) The moment he leaves, she moves the money horde to a new hiding place, wrapping it in another layer of paper – a newspaper with the word "Okay" ironically visible in a headline – and placing it in deliberately plain view (à la Poe's "The Purloined Letter") on a table. At the exact moment when we see the newspaper in close-up, we hear the word "No" from Norman's off-screen mother, who rails at him for bringing a "strange young girl" home for "cheap, erotic" purposes. Marion gazes out the window much as Sam did when he spoke of his ex-wife. Raindrops fall past the glass as Mrs. Bates pointedly mentions food, appetite, and Norman's "guts," or courage – words that equate the sexual, the gustatory, and the digestive/excremental.

For the meal he has prepared, Norman leads Marion into his parlor, adjacent to his office. (Analogously, Marion's bathroom is adjacent to her cabin.) He sits in a chair throughout this scene, sometimes straight and sometimes leaning forward, as if defecating. At the end of this portion of the film, after his voyeurism through the wall hole, he will return to this position, sitting slumped in thought – it isn't clear whose, his or his mother's.

From the meal and its conversation we cut to Marion in her cabin, figuring out how she can finally put the illicit stuff (what's left of it) where it belongs and resume a normal life. The bank's name is prominently shown on her bankbook: First Security Bank of Phoenix, reminding us that "security" and "Phoenix" have many meanings in this film. She tears up her scratch paper, thinks for a while, then enters the bathroom and – in a full close-up unprecedented in Hollywood film – flushes the paper down the toilet, decorously closing the lid after we've had a good look at the paper floating in the water. She removes her robe, commencing her fatal shower, as the toilet noisily finishes its flush.

Entering the bathtub, she draws the shower curtain, a theatrical gesture that closes off two "performances": the crime, of which she has now repented, and the "act" she has unwittingly put on for her voyeuristic observer. She aims a stream of water at herself, and we see it spewing from the shower head, echoing the toilet shot of moments before. There follow three shots of Marion bathing, many of her facial expressions conveying intense, perhaps sexual pleasure. When we see the shower head again, in profile, its phallic shape contrasts with the horizontal pool of the toilet much as Sam's standing body (and Marion's jutting breasts) offset the horizontality of her torso in the film's opening scene.

And then Marion gets killed, in the most celebrated montage of Hitchcock's career. Its most significant aspect may be the fact that its kineticism not only *shows* but *obscures*. That is, we see a great many views from a great many angles; yet far from feeling surfeited with information about the event, we instead feel confused as to exactly what's going on, except in the general sense that Marion is being knifed to death. With its paradoxical suggestion of squeamishness and a bizarre sort of tact in the midst of horrific violence, this is an important consideration about a scene that has been cited, often simplistically, as evidence of misogyny on Hitchcock's part.

The murder scene concludes with another toilet allusion: the bathtub drain with mingled blood and water swirling around it. From this we dissolve to Marion's dead eye, one droplet (or tear) visible near it. The camera pulls back, spiraling in the direction opposite to that of the water. (The opening credits of *Vertigo*, with its eyes and spirals, are echoed here.) Then it retreats directly, as if imitating Marion's departing spirit.

Cut to the shower head, in profile, still gushing. Move from Marion's face, past the toilet, across a white wall (for another "white flash" effect), out the bathroom door, into the bedroom, to a closeup of Marion's newspaper – containing its forbidden load – on a night table. Also on the table is a round, empty ashtray and an erect lampstand on a circular base. With flowing water still audible in the background, the camera continues to the window, through which we see the house in the distance. Norman's voice cries out the only words we hear during this long portion of the film: "Mother! Oh, God! Mother! Blood! Blood!" (This and other moments in *Psycho* can be read, of course, in terms of menstrual as well as excremental anxieties.)

Norman reacts to his "discovery" of the crime by grasping his mouth in a gesture connoting nausea. As he does this, he stands next to the bathroom's open door while directing his eyes away from the room itself. In a film so fascinated by the power of the gaze, and Norman's gaze in particular, this must be read as an attraction–repulsion response (recalling *Vertigo*) related to Hitchcock's strategy of showing/obscuring the shower murder itself. Norman is momentarily frozen between a horrified desire/need to look and an equally horrified fear of looking – a condition immortalized in Michelangelo's vision of *The Last Judgment,* where a particularly poignant soul covers one of his eyes in fright while staring transfixedly with the other at the fate awaiting him. Norman's hand-to-mouth gesture has somewhat different psychodynamic implications, but its message is similar, and his eyes are starkly expressive, especially given the crucial part they have played in the film so far.

Norman's cleanup of the crime is compulsive and obsessive by any standard, yet its motivation is real and clear: to cover all traces of a deed that must be hidden at any cost. Marion's act of larceny and flight also had compulsive and obsessive characteristics, in a different way, and Norman's cleanup echoes certain moments in her portion of the narrative. He has now taken over as protagonist of the film. Again water swirls around a drain, this time in the sink as he washes his hands. Again we see the toilet (but not the shower head, its phallic role perhaps taken over by Norman's male presence) as he swabs and dries the tub and floor. He drops his towel and mop into a round, empty bucket shown in close-up.

Norman pauses in front of the shower head before leaving the cabin. Then he backs the rear of Marion's car to the door and places her corpse (draped in the shower curtain, much as her money is wrapped in paper) into the trunk. The treasure-bearing newspaper is the last of her belongings that he finds and tosses into the car. Ironically, he nearly overlooked what has been the film's most highly charged material, almost leaving it to continue floating indecently around the world. He drives off, the camera cutting to a close-up of the car's rear end and following it to the edge of a swamp.

The swamp is itself a toilet, of course, and one that suits Norman's bigger-than-life psychosis: overflowing with dark, thick gunk that intrudes into the world and is capable of embracing the most enormous, outrageous shit that even Hitchcock's mind could imagine. Horrifyingly, it almost doesn't complete its flush – the car pauses in its descent, threatening not to disappear. Norman waits, nibbles, glances around with a distinctly birdlike gesture, and smiles as it sinks finally into the muck. Sound effects underline the scatology of the scene. Fade to black on the muck.

With this visit to Norman's private cesspool, the motivating money/excrement of the film vanishes for good. We might reasonably expect the narrative to pick up a new symbolic thread as it inherits a new protagonist. But the joke is on us. Norman also has a retention problem with symbolically charged excremental material – that is, material eliciting a social and superego demand that it not be retained, handled, or valued, but rather disposed of in a definitive and psychosocially approved manner.

Norman's illicit bundle – which has started to impose its presence on the film even before the disappearance of the money – is his mother's corpse, which he has refused to mourn, relinquish, and bury in the customary ways. The movie's symbolic order remains entirely intact, its first energizing object impressively exchanged for one far larger, smellier, and more forbidden.

Even if it has disappeared from the movie, however, the $40,000 has not disappeared from the memories of those who knew about it and still survive. After some preliminaries, the film's next movement begins with Sam, Lila, and Arbogast conversing about it. The money makes Marion conspicuous, the detective says, and Lila reveals that Lowery doesn't want to prosecute but only to get his money back. This attitude is consistent with the film's main priority vis-à-vis the money, which is to stress its moment-by-moment location – retained by a "wrong one," in the automobile dealer's phrase, and withheld from its psychosocially "proper" place – rather than its value as a medium of exchange.

It is therefore a search primarily for the money and secondarily for Marion that brings Arbogast to Norman's motel. Hitchcock brings him there in a montage sequence (with a surprising old-Hollywood flavor) that itself reflects the film's preoccupation with retentive and secretive behaviors, and with the repositories around which these behaviors often revolve. When settling into her cabin, Marion's first action was to search the room for a hiding place in which to deposit her forbidden load. Arbogast's discovery of the Bates Motel is shown, analogously, as the climax of a search for the repository that held Marion herself. (The search's montage structure heightens this analogy by condensing the locations visited by Arbogast into a cinematically compact space–time unit, corresponding to the unitary cabin that Marion investigated.) A third search, later in the film, will complete a triad of such activities: the exploration of what Norman calls his "only world" by Sam and Lila, culminating in Lila's penetration of his mother's bedroom, his own bedroom, and finally the fruit cellar where she discovers the secret at the film's core.

The moment Arbogast asks Norman about the house and the person in the window, thus focusing on Norman's mother, their conversation turns to sexuality and sexual identity. The detective suspects that Marion might be using Norman to hide her, and under this pressure Norman insists that he couldn't be fooled "even by a woman." Arbogast answers that he's not insulting Norman's "manhood," and Norman says, "She might have fooled me but she didn't fool my mother." This mother reference is an uncharacteristic lapse on Norman's part, showing how close to the surface of consciousness his guilt (about hiding his physical and mental mother figures) must be.

The irony and the psychology of the scene grow increasingly intricate, and Norman dismisses Arbogast, refusing to let the detective meet his mother. Half in light and half in darkness, Norman watches him drive off. Caged in a phone booth, Arbogast makes a long and visually static call to Lila, saying he will return to the motel. When he enters Norman's office, the camera follows his gaze to Norman's birds and to the safe, which he inspects with the anal attentiveness that marks such passages in this film. Books stand next to the safe, renewing the paper–excrement link associated with Marion's money and newspaper.

The film's anal-obsessive theme has been so elaborately developed by now that Hitchcock doesn't need to lavish very much care on it henceforth. Treatment of this theme thus parallels the film's treatment of physical violence, which deescalates from Marion's murder to Arbogast's and then to the incarceration rather than destruction of Norman himself. Still, the confusion generated among "decent" bourgeois citizens by retention and (mis)handling of forbidden material increases with the sheriff's question of who or what was actually deposited in the local cemetery. Similar confusion will arise from Sam's earnest but hopeless attempt to link Norman with the missing $40,000 in a "rational" way, by ridiculously accusing him of seizing the money in order to build a new motel!

In any case, Norman knows it is time to move his forbidden object to a new location, and the film's signifiers are as logical as they are forthright: He chooses the fruit cellar, a private place associated with organic materials and their processes of ripening and decay. Not his face but his buttocks (swaying effeminately – he is surely "mother" now in thought and identity) address the camera as he climbs the stairs to fetch his treasure. Not for the first time, the screen is split (corridor to right, stairs to left) as he emerges with the corpse and proceeds down the staircase.

The sheriff's wife suggests that Sam and Lila file a missing-person report at dinnertime, which will "make it nicer" – renewing the link between Marion and food. Instead, they return to the motel, conducting the film's last investigation of hiding places and repositories. In the bathroom of Cabin No. 1, shot from a conspicuously high angle, Lila noses around the toilet and turns up a scrap of paper with figuring on it, including a $40,000 notation. Sam, no stranger to obsessiveness himself – one remembers his refusal to marry Marion until his father's debts were paid – immediately deposits the scrap into his wallet, a gesture that mediates between Norman's compulsive cleanup of the bathroom (itself a frantic parody of psychosocially correct activity) and his own urges toward secret (the quest to find Marion without police intervention) and obsessive behavior.

Norman almost catches them as they leave the cabin, but Lila manages to slip away. Sam tells Norman she's taking a nap and that he wants to have a conversation. The camera glances nervously between Lila and the house as she approaches it. (The front door is split by the shadow of a pillar on the porch.) Her investigation takes her into Mrs. Bates's baroque and old-fashioned bedroom, where the fixtures include a dry sink, a cold fireplace, and a dark chandelier, signifiers with precise relevance to Norman's life and the narrative so far. The camera zooms in on a sculpture of two crossed hands. Lila gasps, startled by what turns out to be her own reflection, multiplied to infinity in opposing mirrors. The bed bears the curvilinear impression of a reclining figure, the imprint both of Norman's obsession and of the perceived transgression (by Mother) that propelled it to its full velocity.

Passing to a higher floor, Lila is partly hidden by a bannister that echoes the curved impression in the bed; she then enters a room that seems even more fetishistically determined than Mother's. Apparently frozen since Norman's childhood — and hence a metonymic reference to his paralyzed personality — it contains stuffed animals as well as toys, the *Eroica* on a boxlike phonograph, and a book with no title or author on its cover. (Perhaps this is erotica, and the nearby presence of the *Eroica* is a Hitchcockian joke.) Lila opens the book and gazes impassively for a moment, standing near a little safe and a globe of the world. The atmosphere of both bedrooms is that of a secret world where stasis and retention — paralysis — have always been the rule, rather than movement or transformation.

The sense of paralysis culminates in the climactic scene, dominated by the vision of Mother's rigid corpse. Yet light and shadow dance in her empty eye sockets, which are at once:

a zany and macabre echo of Marion's eye in its moment of final blindness;
a shocking visual pun on the anal and toilet references that have punctuated
   the film; and
a horrible reflection of Norman's urges to retain, to manipulate, to stuff.

The world of stasis and retention finds a second culmination, as well, in the final moments of the film. A "normal" society chooses not to destroy Norman but to stash him into a cold, boxlike repository of its own.

As a whole, *Psycho* is perhaps the most clinical of Hitchcock's films — in the directness and the shamelessness of its subtextual codes — yet also one of his most playful exercises. Hitchcock himself emphasized the latter quality. He called *Psycho* a comedy when I discussed it with him in 1972, explaining that if he had intended a case study, he would have filmed it in a more straightforward style (in the manner of *The Wrong Man,* perhaps) without "mysterioso" touches. Still, the film's clinical implications seem forceful and convincing, leading one to surmise that if Hitchcock regarded *Psycho* as a comedy, it was because, considered through the filter of his own unexemplary emotional development, *any* film dealing with anal retention would be hilarious in a guilty, blushing sort of way.

For all its consistency as a study of this subject, however, *Psycho* refuses to follow a single thematic track. It is also concerned with performance, a constant Hitchcockian interest that is worked out here with special intensity – and a special *interiority* that is, in its way, new for the filmmaker where this theme is concerned.

The "players" in most Hitchcock films remain essentially sure of their own natures and identities during their performance activities. *Vertigo* marks a new step in this area, taking performance beyond the realm of theater-as-strategy and theater-as-metaphor and raising it to a level at once so boundlessly mythic and ineluctably personal that it becomes caught up with the nature of human identity itself.

In the world of *Psycho* – a domain still more extreme – performance is seen as the very *essence* of human identity. Norman gives what is surely among the most flamboyant performances in all of Hitchcock's work. To be sure, it is less physically intimate than that given by Alicia for Alexander in *Notorious* and less physically elaborate than that of Judy as Madeleine in *Vertigo,* with its impeccable costuming, intricately worked-out history, and carefully chosen "location work," all aimed at the most intent and demanding of "audiences." Yet ultimately, Norman's is the most impressive performance because it is the most profound: He alone literally gives himself up to the "character" he plays, assuming not only her voice (in off-screen "conversations"), but also her appearance and costume (the dress he wears during the murders and when we see him through the bedroom window), her movements (the sway of his buttocks as he walks up the stairs), and of course – most drastically – her thoughts.

Hitchcock confronts Norman and his performances in a unique way that is signaled by the treatment of window/curtain imagery. Generally speaking, curtains and windows in Hitchcock indicate the imminence of performance, usually intended for a private "audience" and often not consciously conceived as performance at all, but as "spontaneous" behavior. For different sorts of examples, think of Brandon and Phillip staging their "theater piece" in *Rope,* Uncle Charlie's ordinary-guy masquerade in *Shadow of a Doubt,* and the twin case of Roger Thornhill's forced role as Kaplan and Eve Kendall's voluntary role as Vandamm's lover in *North by Northwest*. Each of these cases (like many others) is associated at some point with the manipulation of curtains, a trope that has the effect of (a) distancing us from the characters as performers and (b) calling attention to the performance-within-the-film that they create. By this double process Hitchcock achieves both a Brechtian alienation effect and a sense of intimacy (fostered also by other devices, including subjective camera work) between the on-screen world and our world as spectators.

Rear Window is another seminal film in this regard. It posits a community of windows, and of the behaviors and communications that such an environment would foster – indeed, nearly all the figures on whom Jefferies spies are performers in some sense, from the "Hunger" sculptress to the dancing Miss Torso, the piano-playing songwriter, the fantasy-enacting Miss Lonelyhearts, and the newlywed couple who "perform" with their curtain drawn. (One critic calls Jefferies's neighborhood a "world of desire."[6]) Upping the ante, *Psycho* posits an entire city of windows – we see it in the opening shots – and suggests that secretive passage through and beyond these barriers (which Jefferies achieves only momentarily and vicariously) is the only way of gaining access to the human and inhuman secrets locked inside. (Hitchcock thought of the opening of *Psycho* as witnessed from a fly's-eye view, the insect being mimicked by the camera.[7])

Psycho has a full share of curtains, drapes, and blinds. Yet it is specifically windows – the transparent surfaces that both divide and connect spatial/visual areas – that are the key factors in defining Norman's relationship to us, to his fellow characters, and to the universe they inhabit. Our first view of Norman is through a window of the house, behind which he parades in his mother's dress. In tropes that link him with his victims and pursuers, we have our first sight of Marion and Sam after passing through the window of their hotel room, and of Arbogast as he gazes through the window of Sam's hardware store. We even see Hitchcock through the window of Lowery's office – ironically distancing himself from the voyeurism of his film by facing *away* from the window, the camera, and the characters. Marion's flight from Phoenix takes place behind the windshields of two cars, through one of which the traffic cop peers, his eyes hidden by unsettlingly opaque "windows" (sunglasses) of their own.

Mirrors provide variations and amplifications of the window motif, folding spatial/visual areas back on themselves while serving as nearly ubiquitous metaphors for the personality splits that characterize Norman (permanently) and Marion (temporarily). In addition, mirrors change people who are only

Figure 12. Windows, reflections, and split subjects: Norman (Anthony Perkins) and Marion (Janet Leigh) in *Psycho*. (Museum of Modern Art/Film Stills Archive. Copyright © by Universal City Studios, Inc. Courtesy of MCA Publishing Rights, a division of MCA, Inc.)

half-captured by the camera (in side view) into whole figures – one profile presented directly to the spectator, the other seen indirectly by reflection (Fig. 12). In a pivotal scene, Norman makes a window out of the wall between his office and Marion's cabin. Mirror imagery also comes into play here: As he gazes through his peephole, the camera moves so close to Norman's eye that we see it (albeit from a profile view) as closely as *he* would see it were he gazing not through a hole at Marion, but into a mirror at himself. On one crucial level, this is exactly what Norman must be doing at this point – turning mentally inward to engage with the full force of his "mother half," which then drives him away from hole, wall, and office to enter the house and prepare for the movie's most momentous action.

It is that action – the killing of Marion – that has kept *Psycho* commentators most busy over the years. Less attention has gone to the movie's last moments. Indeed, although the film achieves some of its greatest intensity during its climax in the fruit cellar, many have accused *Psycho* of sagging badly in its penultimate scene. Yet the psychiatrist's speech is a carefully conceived moment that plays a crucial role in the architecture of the work. The speech serves precisely to bring the film, the narrative, and the spectator down to earth after the shattering events and revelations of Lila's penetration into Norman's secret world. It is indeed a sagging moment – of rationality and psychologizing that are at once glib, tiresome, and oddly comforting in their reassurances that the narrative has after all made sense. One of its chief purposes *is* to sag, so that the next scene will take us all the more by surprise with the profundity of its voyage into the uncharted realm of psychotic evil. If we traveled directly from the fruit cellar to Norman's cell, the effect would be one of unrelieved strangeness and exoticism, allowing us to feel that the world of *Psycho* is utterly disconnected from our own experience. Through the psychiatrist, Hitchcock pulls us relentlessly into a facile, all-too-ordinary reality that we instantly recognize – and in which we feel instantly comfortable – only to plunge us abruptly and irremediably into Norman's world again, this time to emerge only when the film has ended.

In the last scene, Norman/Mother speaks of a fly that crawls across his/her hand; it may remind us of our own flylike entrance through the hotel window at the beginning of the film. At the end of the monologue – a chilling counterpoint to the psychiatrist's lecture – he/she grins, and here one of the film's least prolonged, yet most complex effects takes place: the momentary appearance of a grinning skull (presumably mother's) over Norman's insanely grinning face.

This moment deserves examination since it is a memorable and popular one (often greeted with a vocal response by audiences) that also exemplifies Hitchcock's ability to slide past the ordinary categorizations of classical Hollywood cinema. In one sense it is a dissolve, since the death's-head fades into view over a shot that is already on-screen. But in another sense it is a superimposition, since a dissolve usually effects a transition from one scene/sequence to another, whereas in this case the death's-head does not remain in view (starting a new scene/sequence) after the preexisting image of Norman fades out, but rather dissolves *with* it into the final shot of the swamp and car.

This cinematic event carries forward a great deal of mirror-related imagery that has recurred throughout the film, but does so obliquely. Norman's identification with his mother is an entirely internalized phenomenon that a mirror could not capture; even when he believes he *is* his mother, he would see *his* face when looking into a mirror. Yet his identification with Mother has become so complete that, on a hallucinatory level, her face *is* his face. Our fleeting glimpse of Mother's face over Norman's is Hitchcock's way of conveying the impossible mental contortions in which Norman is now permanently engaged – and conveying these through imagery that is as accessible as it is complex.

This shows that Norman has achieved what Hitchcockian characters sometimes dream of but rarely attain: a state of pre-Oedipal conjunction with an utterly undifferentiated other, in this case the mother-self with whom Norman has consorted for so long.[8] His condition is universalized in the final shot of the film, when the toilet-swamp becomes a birth site, delivering up Marion's corpse (wrapped in the car's rear end, its taillight an ultimate blind eye) umbilically connected to Hitchcock's camera and the world beyond.

Notes

1. Stephen Rebello, *Alfred Hitchcock and the Making of Psycho*. New York: Dembner, 1990, p. 165.
2. Sigmund Freud, *A General Introduction to Psychoanalysis*. New York: Washington Square Press, 1952. trans. by Joan Riviere. pp. 352–3.
3. Ibid., p. 336.
4. During his 1962 interviews with Truffaut, about two years after *Psycho* was released, Hitchcock said he would like to make a movie concerned with food, beginning with "its arrival in the city" and ending with "the sewers, and the garbage being dumped out into the ocean." The film, he added, would show "a cycle, beginning with the gleaming fresh vegetables and ending with the mess that's poured into the sewers. Thematically, the cycle would show what people do to good things.

Your theme might almost be the rottenness of humanity." François Truffaut, with the collaboration of Helen G. Scott, *Hitchcock*. New York: Simon & Schuster, 1984, p. 320.

5. Margaret M. Horwitz, "*The Birds:* A Mother's Love," in *A Hitchcock Reader,* eds. Marshall Deutelbaum and Leland Poague. Ames: Iowa State University Press, 1986, 279–87, cited at 284, 287n.

6. Jean Douchet, "Hitch and His Public." *Cahiers du cinema* 113, Nov. 1960. Reprinted in ibid., pp. 7–15, cited at 8. Trans. by Verena Conley.

7. Rebello, *Hitchcock,* p. 80: "According to a scribble found on a production sheet, Hitchcock was amused by a notion of screenwriter [Joseph] Stefano to sweep the viewer – almost as if he were to become a fly on the wall – into the hotel room window to spy on Sam and Marion, post-tryst." Additional fly references were experimented with during the preproduction period; Norman's final soliloquy contains the most important one to appear in the finished film.

8. See Patrice Petro's statement (citing Julia Kristeva) that "desire is never simply desire for an object... but also for an experience that precedes object choice and sexual differentiation (a desire rooted not in identification but in its dissolution)." Patrice Petro, "Rematerializing the Vanishing 'Lady': Feminism, Hitchcock, and Interpretation," in Deutelbaum and Poague, pp. 122–33, cited at 124.

7
The Birds

It all goes to show that with a little effort even the word "love" can be made to sound ominous.

       – Hitchcock to Truffaut

Much has been made in these pages, as in most Hitchcock criticism, of details – some of them quite small – woven into the visual fabric of his films. As suggested earlier, Hitchcock's work is especially conducive to such close examination because of the care he took in working out that fabric, planning every shot with great precision.

It remains true, of course, that a critic may occasionally (or not so occasionally) launch into what Raymond Durgnat has called a "delirium of interpretation," reading all sorts of meanings into all sorts of details that have quite different significances, or no significances at all. In art as in life, I wish to avoid delirium as regularly as possible, and I don't suggest that every nuance of every Hitchcockian frame is pregnant with undiscovered meaning. Yet sometimes the most bland-looking detail takes on unexpected resonance, and the attempt to discover why can yield more resonances yet, leading one to suspect that Hitchcock might indeed have had something in mind – perhaps even what the critic has in mind – when he composed the image.

Here is one example, embedded in a scene that has more important things going on in the foreground. Well into *The Birds,* heroine Melanie Daniels/ Tippi Hedren has just discovered a large number of probably lethal crows perched on a jungle gym outside a school. As she starts toward the building to warn its occupants, we see still more birds perched in the playground. Melanie enters the building to warn the teacher, Annie Hayworth/Suzanne

Pleshette, who tells the children there's to be a fire drill – thus connecting birds and fire, and foreshadowing the film's most (literally) explosive sequence later on.

As she speaks, Annie is framed by two objects, commonplace for a schoolroom: a portrait of George Washington and a world map. Hitchcock calls no special attention to them. If we focus on them, though, we find they suggest things about the scene that deepen its significance, at least subliminally. The portrait obviously signifies traditional authority and – what would not be the case if it showed, say, the school principal or the local mayor – *dead* authority, present in appearance but not power.

The map is a more complex object. It suggests the possible ubiquity of the spreading bird menace; and, more interesting, it signifies the all-encompassing nature of the feelings (helplessness, terror) felt by the characters at this time. Adults may feel as vulnerable as children when faced with an inexplicable and perhaps ineradicable threat; such fear may be overwhelmingly strong, reaching to the deepest recesses of mind and heart – and all the more so when danger is manifested in such a dreamlike, almost hallucinatory way as happens in this movie. In the film's most powerful moments, such as the jungle-gym sequence, Hitchcock is conjuring up the dark, awful potency of dreams and childhood fantasies, including not only Oedipal castration anxieties, but also pre-Oedipal annihilation fears. Such terrors, in the monolithically structured infant mentality, are undifferentiated from other psychological functions and from reality itself. In a word, they are *global* – hence Hitchcock's suggestive use of outer-world imagery that darkly suggests an all-encompassing inner condition.

The evocation of a link between two modes of being – the *outer* represented through imagery, the *inner* by metaphor and allusion – is characteristic of Hitchcock movies. *The Birds* is perhaps the most loudly debated of them all, dividing critics and audiences into rival camps: those who call it one of his most complex and rewarding achievements, and those who assail not only its performances and allegedly unconvincing character relations, but, more important, its unyielding ambiguity and its insistence on mixing the stuff of everyday life (and movies) with elements of unbridled fantasy.

There is some justice to the anti-*Birds* criticism. Aspects of Hedren's performance are more sterile than stylized, and some moments of potentially rich human interaction (such as the final scene between Melanie and Lydia) are regrettably thin by the Hollywood generic standards that Hitchcock seems (at times) to be invoking in a fairly sincere manner.

The film demands to be explored on deeper planes, however, than those of naturalistic acting and melodramatic verisimilitude. The most strongly felt hostility to *The Birds* centers on the film's temerity in mingling the quotidian with the fantastic, the romantically conventional with the enigmatically unresolved. In bringing these elements together, Hitchcock violates the rules of classical cinematic storytelling in ways that make some spectators distinctly uncomfortable. The essential fact is that he does this for a clear purpose: to call up the sort of all-consuming fantasies and fears that lurk in every unconscious, but are generally toyed with in Hollywood films only – if at all – so they may finally be assuaged by the processes of narrative and cinematic closure.

Hitchcock's career up to the period of *The Birds* may be seen as a trajectory from early experiments with a truly unsettling and disorienting cinema (e.g., *The Lodger,* especially with the guilty-hero ending he wished it to have) through an uneven but often brilliant period of popular entertainments (from the seminal "classic thriller sextet" to *To Catch a Thief*) and films with a truly subversive edge (e.g., *Rope* and *Vertigo*). At the peak of his maturity he made *Psycho,* which seems to have surprised even Hitchcock with its ability to churn up deeply rooted physical and psychological anxieties. *The Birds* is very much a follow-up to *Psycho,* with Hitchcock seeking to go further beyond the bounds of rationality than even Norman Bates's grim adventure allowed. It projects Norman's disequilibrium into the world at large, showing us not an individual but an entire world possessed by madness, confusion, and a rage – erupting not from within but, incredibly, from without – that is as mysterious as it is murderous.

There is no psychiatrist this time, moreover, to intercede between Hitchcock's chaos and Hitchcock's spectators, dispensing words that seem (at least momentarily) to encompass and therefore palliate the vision's savagery. *The Birds* not only depicts the irrational; it *becomes* the irrational by refusing to allow natural (or cinematically naturalized) causal relationships to glue together its hazily separated "real" and "fantastic" elements. Its tricks and tropes, many of them slyly introduced in the guise of conventional melodramatic conceits, often have the effect of "pulling" the narrative away from its seemingly conventional bases (much as an unconventional painting does in *Suspicion,* as Stephen Heath has shown[1]). What makes *The Birds* more radical than other Hitchcock films is its refusal to *return* us to normality by means of standard narrative resolutions. This is the primary source of its power to disorient and disturb. That power is augmented by Hitchcock's ability to inject disorientation and disturbance into the most seemingly innocuous details, such as the decorations in a California schoolroom full of singing children.

To be sure, *The Birds* can be examined on a broad scale, and tantalizing generalities can be posited about it. One might explore it as a tale of air, earth, fire, and water as manifested by (respectively) birds, humanity, explosive danger, and hope of salvation across the water that brings Melanie to Bodega Bay. Or one might read it as the tale of one man and three generations of women, with one of these generations (the man's own) doubly embodied by a (cold) blonde and a (warm) brunette. And so forth. But it is in looking closely at the film's details that one finds Hitchcock at his subtlest – once again employing a host of objects, gestures, colors, and other elements to carry his thoughts and attitudes into a created world of film.

The credit sequence establishes an ominous tone for the movie, as words form in midair against a background of rushing bird shapes, accompanied by wing sounds and ghostly cheeping noises. The narrative itself starts more simply, with a whistle – not a bird's chirping, but what used to be called a "wolf whistle," aimed at Melanie as she walks down the street. It's so ephemeral, and so typical of a "cute" moment in a Hollywood movie, that the spectator hardly registers it. Yet it begins the story on an appropriate note.

Despite the simple vulgarity of the whistle and the simplicity of Melanie's actions in crossing a street and walking down a sidewalk, the first shot has an elaborate mise-en-scène, including an early appearance of Hitchcock's familiar bridge motif as Melanie passes a sign with a picture of the Golden Gate Bridge (shades of *Vertigo*). She pauses with a pleased look when she hears the whistle, evidently not disturbed by – or even mindful of – the gesture's rude, sexist message. Her narcissism and flirtatious nature are plain. The shot's virtuoso camera work also stresses her rapport with the city, and with urban life in general. But the city will not be her primary world in this movie.

The second shot shows birds swarming through the sky. As we know from the title and the advance publicity, these will be the villains of the film – and their first appearance is immediately followed by Hitchcock in his cameo, holding a pair of dogs that prefigure two lovebirds we'll meet in the story (Fig. 13). Once again, the moment of Hitchcock's walk-on does not seem chosen at random: Melanie passes him as she enters a pet shop, immediately after our first glimpse of (menacing?) birds overhead. Later, characters will argue about the cause of violent events that have befallen them. None of their speculations solves the mystery, but we have a clue

Figure 13. Hitchcock's pet shop: The director's cameo in *The Birds*. (Museum of Modern Art/Film Stills Archive. Copyright © by Universal City Studios, Inc. Courtesy of MCA Publishing Rights, a division of MCA, Inc.)

that is denied them. Hitchcock reminds us at the start that his presence and control stand behind all the mysteries to follow.

Melanie goes upstairs in the pet shop, where a saleswoman speculates about a "storm at sea" that might be driving the seagulls inland. Surrounded by squawking birds for sale, Melanie waits for information about a mynah bird she has ordered from the shop. Mitch Brenner/Rod Taylor climbs the same stairs and mistakes Melanie for a saleswoman.

"I wonder if you could help me?" he asks, and while the word "help" is ordinary in this context, it starts their relationship by establishing that he is not self-sufficient, but needs something that this attractive young woman might be able to provide. Continuing, he inquires about lovebirds he'd like to buy for a young relative, specifying that they not be too "demonstrative" or "aloof." This is a humorous moment, but also a significant one, suggesting that Mitch's superego sets precise limits (both upper and lower!) on sexuality.

Pretending to be an employee, Melanie strolls among the cages with him, bantering about whether it's right to keep "poor little innocent creatures"

123

in cages. This is an important issue in Hitchcock's work. We know he often uses birds as symbols of chaos (*Blackmail* and *Psycho* provide powerful examples) and that he also has strong feelings about humans in cages – from innocent Manny Balestrero, wrongfully locked in his cell, to deranged and dangerous Norman Bates at the end of his story – not to mention the other cagelike enclosures (telephone booths, cars, etc.) scattered through his work. *The Birds* combines both motifs. Birds, the creatures most frequently held in cages, represent physical and emotional chaos waiting to assault the tenuous order of the world. Fighting their menace, humans will find themselves caged in objects of their own making, including buildings and automobiles.

Melanie accidentally frees a bird, an event that foreshadows the film's later upheavals and suggests that she may be linked with them. Mitch catches the bird with his hat – making practical use of his "costume," if we see his everyday clothing as part of the everyday "performance" he presents to the world. "Back in your gilded cage, Melanie Daniels," he says to the bird, reinforcing the connection between Melanie and birds that started with the wolf whistle and the bird escape.

He then explains to the real (and perplexed) Melanie that he knows her identity because he's seen her in court, where she appeared because of a practical joke. This joke caused some damage, we learn – specifically, a broken window – and again the detail is not random, but prepares us for the important role that windows (and their fragility) will later play in the story. "I merely believe in the law," Mitch says, asserting the energy of his superego for the second time. Melanie runs downstairs after he leaves, catches sight of his license plate, and calls a journalist friend (who works for the other man in her life, her father) to find out the name of this "adversary." She also orders the lovebirds he wanted to buy.

The next scene begins with those lovebirds. Carrying them in their cage, Melanie gets a funny look from a man in the elevator, and it's a resonant moment: She is linked with him by shots of their feet, echoing *Strangers on a Train,* and his stare vaguely recalls the state trooper in *Psycho,* especially when he trails her down the hallway. He turns out to be friendly, though, telling Melanie she'll have to deliver the birds by going to Bodega Bay, where Mitch lives. Cut to Melanie's foot on her car's accelerator and a shot of the caged lovebirds swaying (a famous sight gag, used somewhat differently in *To Catch a Thief)* as the car twists and turns along the rural highway. Melanie is clearly in control of these birds and is clearly enjoying her wild ride. Hitchcock alternates close-ups of her with long shots of the speeding car.

"I wonder if you could help me," she says to the proprietor of a Bodega Bay store, echoing Mitch's words in the pet shop. We get a good view of the sky as the storekeeper points out Mitch's house, and there's not a bird in sight. Another "cage" makes its appearance, though: In his store, the proprietor is firmly caged in – by a protective mesh on the counter and by the things he sells, which surround and enclose him. A second storekeeper is downright invisible among the towers of things for sale. Business rarely has a flattering appearance in Hitchcock's films – one thinks of confining stores in movies from *Blackmail* to *Psycho,* and of the nasty businessmen who culminate in Strutt of *Marnie.* Here the storekeeper is not a bad person, but he's ahead of the film's other characters in setting up his own protective/ restrictive cage, long before physical danger threatens. In a film that gives Hitchcockian importance to eyes, it's also significant that Melanie uses the phrase "you see" twice in her conversation.

Melanie drives to Annie's home, to verify the name of Mitch's young sister. Annie takes on a knowing expression when she learns Melanie is going to the Brenner house. Facing away from Melanie as they talk, Annie speaks of herself as a tiller of the soil and (in frames punctuated by sensuous red tones) probes for clues to Melanie's relationship with Mitch. The lovebirds increase her suspicions when they start cheeping away; yet despite the clear rivalry between the women, Annie and Melanie remain civil to each other. In subtle and unspoken ways, their relationship is a metaphor for the same forces represented by the birds. Each feels emotions stirring within her, regarding Mitch, and these have enormous potential strength. Yet each keeps her feelings caged up – not by a forceful act of will, but simply by adhering to the ordinary behaviors of a civilized person who has not (yet, at least) been pushed beyond the limits of self-control. So far in this movie, passions have vast possibilities that have not been realized.

Annie leans pensively on her mailbox as Melanie drives away, and a dissolve reveals the depth of the women's still-hidden rivalry: As Annie's face lingers on one side of the screen, a sharp penpoint fades in on the other side, aimed straight at her head – and held in Melanie's hand. Once the dissolve is complete, the camera pulls back to show Melanie addressing an envelope to Mitch's sister. She's still decked out in her fur coat, which underlines the animal nature (and feelings) that have played an important (if implicit) part in the film so far.

She drives to the waterfront, where a puzzled dockworker helps this elegantly dressed urbanite into a motorboat. Her trip across the bay is shown partly in long shot and partly in close-up, as she stops the motor and rows in order to keep her arrival a secret. Chirping and cawing are heard just as she starts to row, but the sky is birdless.

Melanie walks toward the house, tightly framed, the camera cutting restlessly between her and the barn that Mitch has entered. Entering the house, she walks down a Hitchcockian corridor, toward the camera. Then she places the lovebirds and Cathy's envelope in the living room, rips up a second envelope, and returns (away from the camera) down the hallway and back down the dock. This episode is shot with the inflections of a suspense sequence, even though the element of actual suspense – will Mitch catch Melanie carrying out her practical joke? – is minor and mild. The decision to construct the scene this way cannot have been mere habit on Hitchcock's part. It must be stressed that the *point* of this movie is still murky for the first-time spectator and that unresolved situations are hovering over us. Hitchcock capitalizes on this neatly and unobtrusively, giving even a transitional scene the visual trappings of suspense and potential explosion.

Tightly framed with the bomblike hulk of the outboard motor, Melanie turns in her boat to watch Mitch's bewilderment as he discovers the lovebirds and rushes outside to see who brought them. The scene is so engrossing that one may hardly notice when – just as Mitch heads toward the water with binoculars – seagulls start swooping in front of the camera. He jumps into his car and races Melanie toward the dock on the far side. She cocks her head in a distinctly birdlike way, just as a gull sweeps out of the sky and pecks viciously into her head. Her gloved hand, with a fingertip marked by blood from her wound, fills the screen – a danger signal that anticipates the red suffusions of *Marnie* soon to come in the Hitchcock–Hedren collaboration.

Mitch helps Melanie from the boat and into a nearby restaurant, where she and the locals survey each other with mutual bemusement. The camera tilts to an odd angle as Mitch treats his new companion's wound with peroxide; the bottles on a shelf behind them lean precariously, as if they might suddenly slide off and fall. Melanie learns that Mitch is a lawyer and playfully accuses him of wanting "to see everyone behind bars," a remark that summons up Hitchcock's never-waning preoccupation with imprisonment, most recently evoked by the lovebirds.

Melanie disguises the purpose of her visit by claiming that Annie is a friend of hers. Mitch sees through her lie, and they argue about whether she "likes" or "loathes" him. She tells him it's the latter, and that she wrote a letter to this effect, but tore it up. Torn paper is important in Hitchcock's work: Melanie's ripped-up letter recalls that of Judy, hit with vacillating emotions on facing a new relationship with Scottie in *Vertigo,* and Marion's scratch paper in *Psycho,* the only physical trace of her to persist after her death.

Their banter stops when Mitch's mother, Lydia/Jessica Tandy, appears over his left shoulder – immediately framed *between* her son and the new woman in his life. She looms in a slightly low-angle close-up as she speaks to Melanie for the first time, and this shot dominates the next part of the scene. Mother gives a knowing "Oh, I see" when she learns it's lovebirds that link Melanie and her son. Mother and son are then shown (as they will be again) as a couple, in visual opposition to Melanie across from them. Yet to everyone's surprise, the scene ends with a dinner date being set, accompanied by marvelously ironic reaction shots.

The next scene finds Melanie not at Mitch's house but at Annie's, where she cajoles her new acquaintance into renting her a room for the night. Barbed hints about her new relationship with Mitch are accompanied by close-ups that isolate the women in separate frames. Bird cries enter the sound track just as Melanie enters Annie's house, and Annie asks if the creatures never stop "migrating," an exasperated question that could also apply to Melanie's travels. The women gaze toward the sky, in a shot that might have come from a science-fiction epic of the 1950s.

Melanie meets the Brenner family in front of their home. The camera singles out Lydia as young Cathy asks whether the lovebirds are "a man and a woman," renewing the veiled sexual tension of the film. As everyone troops in for dinner, we learn that the local chickens suddenly "won't eat," and this worries Mitch.

The spatial organization of the next scene has subtle effects. We see the whole living room as the characters enter it, spreading out in a way that's more expansive than intimate. A particularly large space remains open between Melanie and Lydia, and Mitch stays mostly in Melanie's territory. When they settle down for drinks, Mitch and Melanie first position themselves on opposite sides of Mrs. Brenner, who's in the foreground; when Mitch moves to Melanie's side, a black lampshade (also in the foreground) remains between them. Like the previous scene, this one concludes with a deliberately static and melodramatic pose that underlines its compositional message: Lydia swings rigidly to look at the telephone while the other two figures (still separated by a small expanse of space) stare in perplexity, and Cathy enters obliviously behind.

Mitch and his mother behave like a husband-and-wife couple in the next scene. Hitchcock separates them from Melanie (playing Debussy on the piano) and from Cathy, who speaks of crime and criminals, then tries to draw Melanie more intimately into the family unit.

Cathy's need for an effective mother is the key to her relationship with Melanie and a clue to the dynamics of the film, which pivots around feelings of lack and emptiness as well as the aggressive jealousy that swirls among the women of the story. Cathy's use of the lovebirds as surrogates for family and friends is an ironic counterpoint to the Hitchcockian view of birds as representatives of chaos and evil. All the characters lack full, supportive families and networks of helpful friends, but only Cathy has the additional helplessness of being a child dependent on adults; hence, she has the greatest void at the heart of her life. She turns to the bird world for solace, and it shows her a token of affection: The lovebirds never share in the destruction wrought by all other birds. Or is their passivity a consequence of their being caged – again like Cathy, who doesn't have the adults' ability to choose options and act on them? Like many things in this endlessly ambiguous film, this is not clear. Hitchcock is consistent in pointing to Cathy as the most vulnerable of all the major characters, however, and the only one with a relationship to birds that is not entirely negative.

Quoting her brother, Cathy likens San Francisco to "an anthill at the foot of a bridge," an unflattering (and animal-oriented) description of a city that Hitchcock has already associated with vertiginous danger and neurosis. (The connection between *The Birds* and *Vertigo* is further strengthened by Rod Taylor's gestures and inflections, which are often similar to James Stewart's in this portion of the film.) Cathy then speaks of a surprise party she's not supposed to know about. In the kitchen, Mitch calls his mother "dear" and "darling," further indicating the almost conjugal nature of their emotional relationship. Yet he simultaneously defends the more conventionally suitable woman who has come into his life, parrying Lydia's questions about Melanie and also her recollection of newspaper reports about Melanie jumping naked into a Roman fountain. ("As naked as a jaybird," one might say, although nobody articulates this.)

Hitchcock dissolves from Lydia's face to Mitch and Melanie together, indicating clearly what's on the older woman's mind. High- and low-angle shots emphasize the predominance of Mitch's physical presence over Melanie's; he looms over her as he asks pointed questions (indeed, cross-examines her) about the Rome incident – she denies she was naked – and her prior relationship with Annie, which Melanie admits she invented. Rejecting his suggestion that they meet again, she zooms off in her car, down a receding roadway under a darkling sky. This is a key moment in the film.

Mitch stands pensively as she drives off, and bird noises – not heard during the conversation and argument – suddenly well up. Glancing to his left, Mitch sees telephone wires covered with birds. More puzzled than alarmed, he walks away.

Annie's rustling newspaper echoes the sound of birds as Melanie enters her living room. In turn, Melanie's next action – removing her coat – visually echoes Annie's gesture. The characters are clearly linked in a tight web of interconnecting gestures, orchestrated by Hitchcock and extending beyond themselves to the natural world.

Melanie sips brandy, undiplomatically says she "despises" Bodega Bay, and listens while Annie confirms her own past relationship with Mitch. Annie also hits the brandy while explaining her theory that Mitch's relationships with women are always stymied by his mother, who – while not "possessive" in the sense of fearing Mitch's loss – resents any woman who could give him the one thing *she* gives him: love.

Annie refers specifically to the Oedipus myth as she rejects the notion that Lydia is jealous and possessive in the classic sense, but – less threateningly – is only afraid of being abandoned. Oedipus is not a new reference point for Hitchcock, whose films (notably *North by Northwest*) have been productively examined in the light of this myth. Annie's mention of it is not a major or fully developed statement, however. It is just a glancing reference that makes the scene more resonant without supplying definitive clues to its meaning. (Along with many other factors, it also serves to distinguish this movie from *Psycho,* in which "mother" is most possessive indeed, albeit in a bizarre and second-hand manner. Then again, Lydia is a bit like Mrs. Bates in that, as Annie sees it, she blocks any relationship with women her son might have.)

Melanie, often associated with culture in the film, is flanked by books and records as she talks with Annie. Mitch calls to ask if Melanie will attend Cathy's party the next day. Melanie agrees and then asks Annie if this was a good decision. Annie says yes, if she *wants* to go. Melanie thanks her, and – at just this moment of rapprochement between the women – a thud is heard from outside. Annie opens the door, and the women find a dead seagull on the porch floor.

Annie says it's a "poor thing" that "probably lost its way in the dark," but Melanie points out a full moon. The women turn their gazes on each other. The night, the sky, and the winding road stretch away between them. This is one of the film's most deliberately artificial tableaux, again illustrating Hitchcock's tendency to underline pivotal moments with obviously ersatz cinematic punctuation – as in *Vertigo,* when Scottie and Judy/Madeleine embrace in front of a crashing sea. Both scenes mark turning points in the emotional and physical lives of the characters, and both are Hitchcockian asides to the audience, reminding us of his presence in the cinematic and narrative processes now working themselves out. Fade to black.

The next shot makes a strong contrast, with its bright lighting and happy view of children playing (safely caged by a white fence) while Melanie and Mitch make their way up a picturesque hillside. Melanie tells about the activities she's taken up as a way of "finding herself" after her dissolute Roman sojourn. "I sometimes go to bird shops on Fridays," she adds, and Mitch hears her joke with pleasure, remarking on the "innocence" of such a day. She tells her plan to give a straitlaced aunt a *talking* bird as a gift – the film's connection between birds and humans is cemented ever more tightly – and says the bird might shock the aunt with improper words, a joking reference to sexuality.

Mitch mentions "a mother's care" and Melanie reacts with displeasure, telling how her own mother "ditched" the family for a love affair. She almost breaks down when admitting that she doesn't know where her mother is – although we don't see her distress, since Hitchcock turns her back to us; even the nape of her neck is covered by an upturned collar. Melanie's bad relationship with her mother is another anticipation of *Marnie,* in which the relationship is less distant but provokes even worse emotional stresses in the heroine.

Melanie is back under control when she turns to the camera again, suggesting with a half-smile that she should "join the other children." The two walk downhill toward the party, the camera preceding them with a moderately paced pan. This finishes on Annie, who has just blindfolded Cathy – an oddly sinister image of fun and games – but herself gazes fixedly at the couple approaching her. Lydia gazes just as intently, and as if to underline this, a child calls, "Look, look!" A bird rushes from the sky and pecks Cathy on the head, in an attack similar to the one Melanie suffered on the boat. More and more birds join the fray, concentrating on children as their victims. Melanie and Mitch gaze in surprise, almost like spectators of the event, before springing into action; at this moment, three of Hitchcock's fascinations – with passivity, with paralysis, and with the consuming nature of the gaze – are woven into a subtly articulated whole.

Becoming fully involved in the battle, Melanie saves a girl undergoing a particularly relentless attack by a single bird. The partygoers take refuge behind a door; it frames them with an orderliness that contrasts vividly with the event we've just witnessed. Annie notes that this is the third bird attack, and Melanie enumerates them. The scene ends with children gazing toward the sky, another image that echoes science-fiction conventions, particularly of the 1950s.

Inside, protective Lydia adjusts the curtains over a window while the lovebirds fidget in their cage. As we have seen, curtains in Hitchcock films often have the dual function of shielding/hiding and of indicating a theatrical dimension to the actions of the characters; here the former predominates but the latter also comes into play, as Lydia briefly acts out her anxiety over the birds' ability not only to attack but to observe (and thereby to locate) her family. Melanie and the others sit intimately in the living room, but Lydia positions herself as far from the younger woman as she can. Mitch's head and shoulders (in the foreground) divide the frame and separate the women. A high-angle shot of Melanie presages the next stunning event: She sights a single bird in the fireplace, followed by an overwhelming rush of birds out of the chimney and into the room. After a good deal of ineffective flailing about, Melanie guides Cathy and Lydia out of the room; then Mitch leaves too.

In the aftermath, the living room is very much like a stage set (following up the curtain business a little earlier) that has been meticulously arranged to simulate disorder. A deputy sheriff, visiting the house, has only painfully obvious things to say about the incident; he is of no more real help than the sheriff in *Psycho*. Lydia picks up a shattered china teacup, a favorite Hitchcock symbol; Melanie follows her actions carefully with her eyes. A dead bird falls and shocks Lydia, just as she straightens her late husband's portrait on the wall. She swings pensively toward the camera again, as Melanie and Cathy go to fetch Melanie's things from the car.

The next scene opens with a long shot of a large, empty expanse (only Mitch is visible in the distance) formally framed by a sort of trellis outside the house. Hitchcock is again greeting the most disorderly events with conspicuously ordered cinematics. Inside, dressed in virginal white, Melanie puts finishing touches on her makeup and costume, as if preparing for the next scene in a drama. Ironically, though, Lydia will star in this episode. In extreme long shot – the kind of shot associated with birds in this movie, and with the filmmaker's detachment – we see her pickup truck approach a neighboring farm. As she enters the house, her gaze is arrested by a row of smashed teacups; the neatness of the row attests to Hitchcock's compulsive control, just as its shattered components (the individual cups) manifest the horrific chaos he is portraying here.

Moving on, she enters a corridor that seems cramped, airless, and endless, even by Hitchcock standards. Looking into a room, she sees a still life of wreckage and chaos. A third point-of-view shot discovers the farmer's naked feet beneath ripped trouser legs. Lydia then sees the man's lifeless face, in a series of three increasingly tight shots that zero in on his empty eye sockets (vividly recalling Mrs. Bates in *Psycho*). Her own mouth gaping just as widely, emptily, and silently, Lydia flees down the corridor toward the camera, her motions like those of a panicky bird. The shot lingers for an instant after she leaves it, and the next shot starts before she enters the frame, reinforcing the emptiness that characterizes this sequence. She runs down a walkway toward a bewildered workman, her mouth still gaping but with only strangled gasps coming out. In another extreme long shot, her truck races back down the road, spewing a wake of smoke and dust that wasn't visible during her earlier trip. (This recalls another horrific signifier: the thick, artificially created smoke that gushed from the locomotive of Uncle Charlie's train early in *Shadow of a Doubt*.) She spills out of the truck, stands gasping between Mitch and Melanie, then tears herself away and races into the house.

Melanie seems quite contained as she prepares tea for Lydia. She and Mitch embrace and kiss as they warn each other to be careful; their intimacy, both emotional and physical, is growing, which may explain Melanie's calmness in the preceding moments. She serves Lydia in bed, and Lydia worries about Cathy at school, explicitly connecting the broken windows at the nearby farm with the large, vulnerable windows at the school. (The connection between windows and eyes, especially the plucked-out eyes of the farmer, is strong but not explicit.) Opening up to Melanie, Lydia speaks with surprising directness about her affection for her late husband and admits her ambivalence toward Melanie herself. She only loses control at the thought of being left alone in the world. Melanie comforts her, albeit with a minimum of physical contact – the physical connection she has established with Mitch does not extend to his mother – and offers to fetch Cathy from the school.

The children are singing, under Annie's direction: "With every stroke she shed a tear," goes the first clearly audible line. Again there is a strong anticipation of *Marnie*, where the words of a children's jingle also have significance beyond the seeming nonsense of their nursery-rhyme framework. This is an effective moment apart from the lyrics, moreover, as the vulnerable kids chirp away *like birds* in their unformed, nearly tuneless voices.

Melanie signals to Annie, then goes outside to wait. Her green suit is conspicuously framed by the red-orange of the school's door – a large, forbidding door that signifies Hitchcockian institutional paranoia; is there a convincing instance of institutional effectuality in any Hitchcock work?

Melanie walks away from the school and sits down; a jungle gym dominates the frame behind her. Exactly when she reaches into her purse for a cigarette, a blackbird flutters onto the jungle gym. Cut to Melanie from another angle, the jungle gym now invisible. Melanie lights her cigarette, and another cut reveals four birds perched on the jungle gym. Cut to Melanie, then to the jungle gym with a fifth bird arriving. Cut to Melanie smoking, then a couple more birds landing. Cut to Melanie still smoking, and looking impatiently over her shoulder in the wrong direction. Then, following her gaze, cut to a single bird swooping through the sky. It goes some distance and lands on the jungle gym, which now holds a frightening number of birds.

This sequence demonstrates Hitchcock's mastery of montage not only as a means of showing and connecting, but also of hiding and discontinuing. It demonstrates the ineffectuality of Melanie's gaze, as well, which failed to see the danger until it had become great and terrifying. Such ineffectuality would be a severe handicap in any Hitchcock film, but all the more so in a movie that situates its danger in the sky, a part of the environment that's accessible to humans through sight above all other senses.

Also striking is Hitchcock's willingness, once again, to assert his authorial control over the protagonist – to pull the strings, in trickster terminology, with unhidden enthusiasm. His handling of vision here, however, is quite different from that in his previous film. In *Psycho*, the impedance of Marion's vision came from natural causes (rain and nighttime darkness) during her drive; from conventional causes (water and shower curtain) during her time of greatest vulnerability; and from derangement and evil (destroying all bodily functions) during her murder. In the *Birds* scene we've just witnessed, Melanie fails to see danger simply because she's looking – courtesy of the filmmaker – in the wrong direction. Our visual information is privileged over hers (i.e., we are allowed more awareness than Melanie of what's going on), but not by much, since Hitchcock causes the threat to creep up incrementally during the temporal discontinuities of his montage sequence. Like the heroine, we are visually and narratively at his mercy, a situation he heartily exploits. (Another disruption of Melanie's vision, forcefully imposed from the outside, will figure importantly in a later bird-attack scene.)

After the schoolroom scene discussed at the beginning of this chapter, a long take shows the birds growing increasingly agitated – an effect achieved largely by the sound track – and then abruptly taking off. Cut to a long shot of the children running down the road toward the camera, the birds swarming overhead. In a complex montage, individual birds swoop in to attack; close-ups emphasize the overwhelming physicality of contact between them and the children. (The shattered eyeglasses of one girl recall certain Eisenstein tropes in *Battleship Potemkin*.) Melanie and Annie rescue this child and Cathy, helping them into a parked car, where they are trapped but momentarily safe. Melanie honks the horn loudly, and this causes the birds to cease their attack. Or does it? Perhaps the time for the attack has passed, and the birds are simply ready to withdraw.

The next scene finds Melanie on the phone in a local bar. The place has large windows that facilitate seeing outside, continuing the film's use of windows as a metaphor for eyes and for the concept of fragility. (Glass plays an important role in this portion of the film. Note the cigarette-machine mirror in the bar, for instance, and the phone booth and automobile that Melanie will hide in.) Slightly offbeat camera angles suggest that things are not as they should be in Bodega Bay, even though the bird attack has ended.

A drunk lounges at one end of the bar. A crusty-looking woman named Mrs. Bundy (her name recalls Mrs. Grundy, the generic nickname for prudish and censorial people) interjects herself into Melanie's conversation, insisting on the strong difference between crows and blackbirds. Continuing her unsolicited lecture on speciation, she prepares to smoke a cigarette – echoing Melanie's habit (which signals a similarity between the two women, who otherwise appear very different) and foreshadowing a fiery eruption that will soon take place. She insists that no bird species would have "sufficient intelligence" to launch an organized attack. Her biological chatter and Latin terminology seem irrelevant to Melanie, compared with the real horror of the attacks. Meanwhile, a waitress (who somewhat resembles Patricia Hitchcock, the director's daughter and occasional actress in his films) hovers around the back of the frame, casting odd looks toward the speaker. She is a clear surrogate for Hitchcock, who uses her to mock the pretentious bird expert: She interrupts Mrs. Bundy's wrong-headed defense of birds by hollering a food order – for fried chicken, of all things.

Mrs. Bundy shifts from defending birds to criticizing human beings. "It's the end of the world," the drunk chimes in, and the waitress orders two Bloody Marys, continuing her encoded commentary. The drunk persists in his biblical mode by quoting Ezekiel, only to be countered by Isaiah on the evils of strong drink. Just as Mrs. Bundy pointedly uses the word "war," a new arrival enters. He turns out to be the most bellicose individual present, suggesting that humanity take up guns and wipe birds off the face of the earth, since most are scavengers, and messy to boot.

This man will soon touch off the film's most flamboyant disaster, and Hitchcock's portrait of his personality prepares us for this role. His drinking is not "cute," as the drunk's is, and he smokes aggressively phallic cigars instead of the more delicate cigarettes associated with the women; in sum, the signifiers connected with him have a distinctly sleazy aura about them, even by saloon standards. His comments give Mrs. Bundy an opportunity to reveal that birds outnumber people overwhelmingly on our planet. Hitchcock, not content with terrorizing Bodega Bay's citizens, here makes it plain that the danger of mutilation and annihilation is literally global, although his narrative approach remains microcosmic throughout the film. (He eliminated shots of bird-caused chaos in the outside world – on the Golden Gate Bridge, specifically – from the final cut of the movie.)

An anxious mother tries to shield her children from the talk as they eat lunch; her son asks if birds are going to eat *them*. (The revenge of the fried chicken?) Ironically, the mother proceeds to alarm her daughter more than the conversationalists did, becoming overwrought and advising everyone to expect the worst. The family leaves with the bellicose man, who has offered to lead them to the freeway. By now Mitch has arrived. Still biblical, the drunk states that birds are sustained by God, and Mrs. Bundy admits that some gulls "lost in the fog" caused damage to another town on an earlier occasion.

And so the conversation goes. Hitchcock has never been generous in his view of language – an attitude stretching through all his sound films – and rarely has he exceeded this scene in demonstrating the uselessness of mere talk. In the same vein, Mitch tries to mobilize a counterattack against the birds, describing an idea about "making fog" to confuse them; but it sounds surprisingly lame (especially from the supposed hero of the film!) and further bears out the futility of words in this desperate situation.

Bird noises enter the sound track even as Mitch outlines his feeble plan. Then, nearby, a service-station attendant is felled by a swooping gull, an event we witness through the cafe's window. (This shot has a Norman Rockwell–style composition, underlining Hitchcock's ironic double view of Bodega Bay as idyllic town and disaster site.) Mitch and others run to the man's aid – struggling against the tide, since the distraught mother and her children run *in* as they exit.

The camera singles out gasoline flowing from a hose dropped by the attendant, then a stream of gas running across the pavement to a wheel of the bellicose man's car. These shots alternate with views of Melanie and others gaping at the scene from the window, where their enforced passivity echoes *our* enforced passivity: Characters and audience are united as mere spectators to the horrendous event. The bellicose man begins to strike a match for his cigar, and Melanie articulates the awful danger he's in – calling it to everyone's attention behind the window, then trying to warn the man. In a dark Hitchcockian joke, the man hears their calls without understanding them – again, language fails. He pauses in lighting the cigar, burning his fingers. This leads him to drop the match, touching off an inferno as flames streak along the gasoline trail to the service station's tanks.

The gasoline explodes, engulfing the man in flames. The image recalls *Saboteur,* containing one of Hitchcock's most harrowing death scenes. The sequence also recalls Hitchcock's often-stated distinction between "surprise," when the audience is merely startled by an effect, and "suspense," when the audience squirms with anticipation because of information that has been deliberately provided; here Melanie announces that the man is lighting a cigar, alerting us to the imminent danger so we can savor its approach as well as its arrival.

We see the events in a fast montage that alternates the action with virtually still shots of the horrified spectators. This has two effects: freezing these characters in a stasis of paralyzed fear and virtually engulfing them in flames along with the explosion victims. Then, in one of the most memorable moments of Hitchcock's oeuvre, the camera is suddenly high in the sky, looking down (literally a bird's-eye view) at the flames. After a long pause, a single gull flies into view – then another, then more, heading toward the fire.

Back on the ground, Melanie and others are attacked as they run out of the building. She takes refuge in a phone booth, another enclosure (like the automobile) that offers some protection yet isolates her and renders her powerless. Another overhead shot, from slightly above her head, emphasizes her caged condition; a car nearly slams into the booth, adding human to avian danger. A brief close-up shows her hand on a window of the booth, trying to ward off the birds, a gesture recalling Marion's effort to ward off Norman in *Psycho.*

Firefighters arrive, in another shot that – except for the violence and weirdness of the situation – has a quaint, old-fashioned quality not unlike that of Rockwell's paintings. As they attack the fire (and birds) with their hoses, water from an out-of-control hose blurs Melanie's vision inside the booth. Again a Hitchcockian woman is crippled by a loss of vision, as Melanie was through inattention in the schoolyard scene, as Marion was during her drive in the rain and again in the shower, and as Marnie will be during the seizures that flood her gaze with overwhelming scarlet tones.

Such blindings, generally inflicted on women rather than men, reflect Hitchcock's concern with actual and virtual paralysis: A blind figure in his films (with occasional exceptions, such as the intuitive blind man in *Saboteur*) cannot make effective movement or take effective action. Blindness can take many forms, moreover, from the tunnel-caused darkness in *The Lady Vanishes* to the hungover haze and topsy-turvy perspective that afflict Alicia in *Notorious*. Impaired effectiveness of vision echoes across the years in Hitchcock films, linking Alice White in *Blackmail* and Margot Wendice in *Dial "M" for Murder* as they grope for weapons that their assailants prevent them from seeing. Melanie's water-induced blindness is momentary and partial, but it is also a forerunner of more profound disability to come; like Marion's drive through the rain, Melanie's stay in the phone booth is a harbinger as well as a dramatic passage.

Complementing the blurred visual component of this scene, the bird noises on the sound track are highly artificial, more like rocket noises (with descending pitch glides) than natural sounds. Two galloping horses, pulling a wagon, add to the chaos and vaguely old-fashioned atmosphere of the moment. Then comes another overhead shot, followed by a strange encounter between Melanie and a man attacked by birds outside the booth: a two-shot of both figures, a closeup of the man's bloody face, a quick montage of him and Melanie, and then he's gone. A bird smashes into a wall of the booth, breaking it. Just as Melanie opens the door (in a distant long shot) to escape, Mitch – in a characteristic Hitchcock miracle – appears at just the right instant to shield her.

They move along a wall and into the restaurant. The bar is positioned diagonally, like the wall we have just seen; more attacking birds are visible outside the large window. People huddle in the room, looking like refugees from a war. Devastated by the birds' behavior, Mrs. Bundy cannot bring herself to face the camera. With mournful and accusatory expressions, others look at Melanie and the camera, as if it shares her blame. They could be right about the link, except "blame" should not be the operative concept.

The mother articulates their thoughts by saying the trouble started when Melanie arrived in town. "Who are you? What are you? Where did you come from?" she ontologically demands, as if Melanie were a devil or monster. Finally she shrieks the word "evil" in Melanie's face. The two are seen in shot–reverse-shot structure until Melanie slaps the other woman; then Melanie appears in a two-shot with Mitch, once again liberated into his protective company. Joining the birds outside, the camera shows the onlookers again gazing through the window. Mitch and Melanie run toward the school down a country road, in an archetypal shot that frames them amid ground, building, and sky as if they were lovers fleeing some disaster in an ancient, mythical time.

The school looms menacingly (recalling the Bates house) as they approach it. Out back, crows are massed again on the jungle gym and swings. The camera nervously shifts its glance from people to birds and back, then to Annie's house. As it swings past the fence we see her sprawled body in front, its legs elevated and apart as if some horrible rape had taken place. (The fence constitutes a particularly striking example of what William Rothman calls the //// motif in Hitchcock's work.[2])

Cathy appears at the front-door window, and although she is cut off from the others by a fragile pane of glass, her face is fully visible – unlike Annie's, which Mitch hides with his hand. The window and Cathy are shown from a low angle as if they were upstairs, so it's a bit surprising when Mitch opens the front door and she rushes instantly into his arms. Melanie stops Mitch from throwing a stone at birds perched on the roof – it's not clear whether she dreads stirring up the situation or feels some strange, residual concern for the birds – and instead he covers Annie's body with his jacket. Echoing this shot, Melanie holds and shields Cathy, her back mostly hiding the girl from the camera while Mitch carries Annie's body inside.

The next shot formally frames the house with Melanie and Cathy to the right, Mitch coming out the front door near the center. He joins the others and walks with them to the road. As if to counter the fear and chaos that have come to dominate the film, Hitchcock now begins to take special care in arranging the characters with geometric precision: Here the tops of their heads form a diagonal line across the screen, since each figure is a different height. They then enter Mitch's car, where Cathy tells a tearful tale.

Dissolve to the boarded-up Brenner house, where Mitch and Melanie are barricading an upstairs window. Mitch comments on the episodic nature of the attacks, and Melanie reports that the phone is dead: Spoken language is losing its potency on yet another level. Lydia calls out that news is available on the radio, however. "Suspect" is the first word we hear from the broadcast as Mitch and Melanie enter the room, which is rigidly framed in the pattern of a cross: Lydia and Cathy in the left and right foreground, respectively, with Mitch completely hiding Melanie's body as he walks toward the camera down the middle. Again the characters are arranged in a precise pattern; the motif of a body being hidden or shielded is also repeated.

Melanie appears in the middle of the room and positions herself on Cathy's side of the frame. The radio report is sketchy and inadequate, true to the narrative's ever-diminishing faith in spoken words. Still enmeshed in conventional language patterns, however, Lydia asks a series of "what if" questions, forcing Mitch to respond that he doesn't know the answers – the hero caught for a second time (after his ridiculous "fog-making" speech) with no words of value to offer.

Lydia becomes upset and Cathy does the same in response, whereupon

Lydia bursts out with, "If only your father were here!" This makes explicit the film's Oedipal tensions. Everyone freezes: Mitch opposite Lydia in a tight shot, Cathy between them. The camera pulls away as Lydia apologizes, revealing Melanie in the rear of the frame, her back to the camera. The group leaves the room in twos, Mitch and Melanie going out the back door and watching a flock of birds flying inland. Fade out on Melanie's face.

Fade in on Lydia, in long shot and mostly hidden by the brunette wood of the piano. Melanie and Cathy are together in the center of the room, some distance away; Mitch is separated from everyone, firming up a barricade on the right. The camera pans to discover each of them in turn, stressing emotional as well as physical distance. Then it follows Mitch around the room, cutting briefly to Cathy when she asks permission to bring in her lovebirds. Standing on Lydia's side of the room, Mitch supports her objection to this, then looks at the lovebirds after checking the kitchen fortifications. Back in the living room, a large distance remains between Mitch and his mother on the left, Melanie and Cathy on the right. Lydia removes some teacups, then returns. Silence. Cathy feels sick and briefly leaves, Melanie with her. When they return, the camera angle emphasizes the portrait of Mitch's father, between Mitch and his mother on their side of the room.

Amid these visual articulations of family dynamics, chirping and rustling are heard. Cathy runs to Lydia, who clutches her. Mitch adds logs to the fire, fending off danger with the same element that *attracted* it during the gas-station episode. Melanie cowers on the sofa, drawing her legs up, increasingly hysterical despite the perfect-as-ever neatness of her hair and suit. Mitch struggles with a bird that has crashed through the window. Beaks peck through the door. We see Melanie from overhead – this is a signature shot for her terror in the film – and then from an oddly low angle. Mitch pulls the shutter closed and secures it with a lamp cord. Seen from overhead, he goes to cowering Lydia and Cathy, leading them to an armchair and leaving Lydia with her hands crossed over her chest, almost corpselike.

Pausing briefly with Melanie, he enters another room. Down a corridor we see the front door giving way to pecking beaks; Mitch moves a heavy furniture piece (containing a glass mirror) to block it, nailing it in place as Melanie watches from the hallway. As the birds and their sound begin to leave, each of the three adults is shown in a separate, identically structured close-up: First we see the ceiling (alluding to the space above the room, including the bird-infested sky), and then a figure moves into low-angle view. Lydia's shot comes last, continuing as the camera pulls slowly back to show all three arranged in a diagonal line (Lydia in the rear and now separated from the others) through the deep domestic space. This scene has been wordless until Mitch's brief "They're going." Its spatial complexities are enormously expressive.

A dissolve superimposes flames on the fading-out faces of Mitch and Melanie; in Lydia's part of the frame, there appears the empty space between the legs of an andiron. Logs slump to the bottom of the hearth, and we cut to Lydia slumped drowsily on the piano bench. Pan to Melanie, then Cathy, then Mitch, spread as far as possible from one another; then a close-up of Melanie as she hears a fluttering of wings. Mitch is asleep – one arm curled in the position of Rodin's *Thinker,* the other hand protecting his groin. He doesn't hear Melanie's soft attempt to catch his attention.

Grasping a flashlight by its large handle, an indication that she is taking on actual and symbolic (phallic) control of the situation, Melanie checks on the quiet lovebirds, then looks toward the stairway. The camera cuts between her and the stairs as she ascends, and lingers on her turning of the doorknob. It then cuts rapidly to a hole in the roof, Melanie's gaping (gasping) mouth, and the shining head of the flashlight.

This sequence is a carefully orchestrated medley of Hitchcockian motifs, beginning with the staircase, a prototypical object with many associations including those of *Psycho.*[3] The flashlight, waving uselessly in the air during the ensuing bird attack (Fig. 14), recalls Mrs. Bates's light bulb, the Statue of Liberty's torch in *Saboteur,* the cigarette lighter in the *Birds* gas-station scene, and other examples of light sources that fail to provide healing illumination. Most pungently, the quickly cut close-ups – hole in roof, gaping mouth, head of flashlight – are a trilogy of Hitchcockian voids, closely associated with the physical and spiritual black holes that yawn amid so many of his films, signaling an emptiness that is ironic at best and terrifying at its frequent worst.

Birds come perilously near Melanie's eyes and other exposed parts of her body. She gasps a useless warning about saving Cathy, then collapses. Mitch arrives with Lydia, barely getting the door open because Melanie's body has slumped in front of it; her paralysis becomes his. He claws at her body, in gestures that would appear menacing under different circumstances, then drags her away much as Scottie drags Judy in *Vertigo.* Lydia, who has bravely accompanied Mitch, takes a nonelectric lamp and leads her son (carrying Melanie) downstairs.

Regaining consciousness on the sofa, Melanie fends off imaginary birds until Mitch stops her, folding her hands on her chest in the same mortuary-style position that he gave to his mother's hands earlier. Mitch revealingly

Figure 14. Blind fear: Melanie (Tippi Hedren) under attack in *The Birds*. (Museum of Modern Art/Film Stills Archive. Copyright © by Universal City Studios, Inc. Courtesy of MCA Publishing Rights, a division of MCA, Inc.)

soothes women by disposing of their hands in a way that hints at symbolic killing, and certainly emphasizes passivity and stasis.

Melanie has reached a state of mental paralysis in any case, unable to speak or act in a meaningful way. In a film that lacks a single and definitive climax, this moment of virtual paralysis for the heroine must be seen as the goal of the narrative so far, and also the pivot on which it will turn in order to approach closure. This movie will have no conventional closure, however; all that remains is for a partially reordered relationship among the characters to allow the emergence of a pathway that *might* lead to a healing of spirit and regaining of potency after the narrative has ended. (Such a postponement of resolution has occurred in Hitchcock before, with sundry variations, notably in *The Wrong Man* and *Vertigo*.)

Determined to take Melanie to a hospital, Mitch opens the front door, seeing a huge quantity of birds framed precisely through an opening in the fence; shafts of dim sunlight add to the preternatural atmosphere. One bird bites his hand, but the others leave him alone as he gets Melanie's car from the garage – hearing on the radio (in a small return of verbal potency) that Bodega Bay is the center of the attacks, although smaller skirmishes have occurred elsewhere.

He and Lydia guide Melanie outside, despite her understandable hesitation about mingling with the birds. They help her into the car in an extreme high-angle shot, and Mitch goes back to fetch Cathy, who asks if she can bring the lovebirds. They "haven't harmed anyone," she says. Are the lovebirds quiet because of the symbolism their name embodies, or simply because they're caged and cannot join the others? It is unclear, but they are allowed to join the human refugees.

Melanie and Lydia smile at each other through their distress. In the car, the family is physically closer than it normally was in the house. It proceeds down the road in a bird-dominated long-shot. Earlier in the film, automobile travel seen in long-shot seemed an echo of bird flight in the distant sky; now the gradual motion of the car reflects the spellbinding power of earth-bound birds that motionlessly surround it. Objects on the left and a tree on the right transform the final shot into a tunnel view – a last evocation of claustrophobia, but perhaps also a sign that Melanie will find the pathway to wholeness that she desperately needs. The sound track fills with bird noises, punctuated by electronic shrieks.

Why does *The Birds* end on such an open and unresolved note? The conclusion of the film – and the conclusion of what many observers regard as the most heroic period of Hitchcock's career – may grow directly from the distrust of language that we have noted as a motif of *The Birds,* in which spoken communication is of little use and even the hero sounds foolish when called on to articulate solutions to the crises of the story. Hitchcock inaugurated his sound-film career by worrying aloud that dialogue might displace "the technique of the pure motion picture," and despite the importance of carefully crafted screenplays to his oeuvre he remained a scopophile rather than a logophile – there is no Hitchcock film, for instance, in which words loom as importantly as images do in *Rear Window* and *Vertigo,* among other vision-obsessed works.

This tendency veers into logophobia in *The Birds,* which is *about* the futility of language. The more its characters talk among themselves, the more extreme their problems become. By contrast, birds cannot talk, write, or use language in any way that a human could identify; yet they seem ever more organized and unified in the narrative. This pattern accounts for some of the film's boldest strokes, as when Melanie and the others make their final escape only when Melanie loses the power of speech (and effective movement) after a particularly traumatic bout with the birds.

On a more sweeping level, the movie's lack of a conventionally resolved ending signals Hitchcock's ultimate gesture of despair over the power not only of words but of screenwriting and storytelling itself. His tale is not yet concluded by any traditional standard: The protagonists are still in danger, their antagonists are stronger than ever, and the emotional relationships of the characters are only partially and tentatively untangled. Yet at this moment Hitchcock, like Prospero, abjures his powers of magic and language making. And it is the resulting visual and narrative stasis that mysteriously allows his characters to grope their way toward – if not actually to enter – a better world. Mitch's futile attempts at verbal solutions to the crisis foreshadow the film's outcome, making him as strong a surrogate for the filmmaker as Scottie or Jefferies ever was. Hitchcock's last classic film thus pivots on the simplest and most revelatory of equations. Mitch = Hitch.

Notes

1. Stephen Heath, "Narrative Space," originally in *Screen* 17, Autumn 1976, 19–75; reprinted in *Narrative, Apparatus, Ideology: A Film Theory Reader*, ed. Philip Rosen. New York: Columbia University Press, 1986, pp. 379–420, cited at 379.
2. William Rothman, *Hitchcock – The Murderous Gaze*. Cambridge, Mass: Harvard University Press, 1982, p. 33 and passim. Rothman says this motif signifies Hitchcock's "mark on the frame, akin to his ritual cameo appearances" as well as "the confinement of the camera's subject within the frame and within the world of the film," and is also "associated with sexual fear and the specific threat of loss of control or breakdown."
3. Brill's thesis about Hitchcockian ups and downs notwithstanding, Melanie's climb is certainly an *ascent* to horror. See Lesley Brill, *The Hitchcock Romance: Love and Irony in Hitchcock's Films*. Princeton, N.J.: Princeton University Press, 1988. Passim.

8

Epilogue

There is a consensus among critics that *Topaz* and *Family Plot* are not up to the standard of Hitchcock's best work, and while *Frenzy* has many admirers, others will accept the judgment that it is more a fascinating near miss than a fully realized success. Yet many connoisseurs would dispute the notion that *The Birds* is Hitchcock's last essential work. *Marnie*, his subsequent film released in 1964, delights most Hitchcockians as much as it disappoints most "Hitchnockians."

I find that *Marnie* grows in stature with repeated viewings, notwithstanding Donald Spoto's revelations about Hitchcock's troubled state of mind during the period when it was made.[1] In ways, it is a lesser achievement — cinematically, philosophically, mythically — than *The Birds*, which itself grows more impressive over the years. Yet just as clearly, it forms a late-period diptych with *The Birds*, not least because of Tippi Hedren's presence in both as the embodiment of some of Hitchcock's most melancholic thoughts on femininity and its place in the world. So it seems appropriate that *Marnie* should have the last word in this study, if not the last full-fledged chapter.

If the heroine of *The Birds* reaches a state of near paralysis at the end of her narrative, Marnie *begins* her story that way. Melanie has squandered much of her time on frivolities (jumping into Roman fountains) and "constructive" activities with no particular purpose; yet she is a spiritual dynamo compared with Marnie, whose thieving and lying fail to satisfy her own desperate longings, much less the imperatives of society as represented by Strutt and other hostile forces.

Her spiritual stasis creeps into the physical world through her inability to have sexual relations and through other manifestations of immobility: She refers to her "paralyzed legs," for example. The stasis afflicting her is contagious, moreover. When she tries to rob the Rutland safe near the end of the film, she is unable to place her hand on the money in front of her, and when Mark attempts to force the matter by guiding her hand, both characters find themselves frozen in the middle of the act. (This recalls *Rear Window,* when Jefferies's helpless immobility is translated to Lisa, trapped by his inattention in Thorwald's apartment as the murderer approaches.)

As often happens in Hitchcock, paralysis is also related to blindness. During the stateroom scene when Mark begins to force his sexuality on Marnie, her eyes gaze (in close-up) blankly ahead, as unseeing as Marion Crane's after Norman's more vicious attentions. Here we again recall Melanie, blinded by forces as different as blasting water hoses and her own lack of alertness.

Marnie and *The Birds* part company in a crucial area, however. What's most important in *The Birds* is not the heroine's inner life but the overwhelming physical danger that suddenly infests her world. By contrast, the central issue in *Marnie* is the heroine's arrested development, signaled by everything from her (sometimes) childish speech patterns to the actual children who chant morbid rhymes in the street outside her mother's house.

The evocation of this condition is an important reason for Hitchcock's use of rear projections during horse-riding and automobile-driving scenes – a device that is noteworthy not for its presence (such process photography is common enough), but for its obviously artificial quality. These projections have been roundly criticized by those who scorn *Marnie,* especially in equestrian shots that plainly lack the muscular sense of liberation that the screenplay (on a superficial level) might lead one to expect.

It is true that Hitchcock's employment of rear projection is not entirely consistent here, since Marnie's artificial-looking shots are intercut with quite vigorous and real-looking views of people on horseback; the essential point, however, is that Marnie's shots are visual echoes of her inability to find needed liberation even in her favorite activity. She suffers from an anhedonia, to cite one of Woody Allen's favorite concepts, that is self-generated – a fact that points to her superego (rather than her id) as the psychodynamic villain in her life, long before the confirming revelations in the movie's second half. A similar point might be made about Melanie, with her inability to allow herself any but feeble substitutes for meaningful intellectual, cultural, and sexual activity.

Marnie and Melanie are both "performers," of course, but in this area Marnie is again a more extreme character. Melanie's performances are brief and whimsical – her impersonation of a shop employee is suggested by Mitch's mistake rather than her own imagination, for example, and her instinct for costuming is weak, as we see from her incongruous urban appearance during the early stages of her Bodega Bay excursion. Marnie, by contrast, is a vigorous actress. Not only does she take on a convincing new role for each new "job" she pulls; more profoundly, her neurosis is a matter of performance – deluding herself as well as others – in its own right, designed to mask realities (particularly that of her violent act as a child) with appearances that ultimately prove sadly inadequate.

Mark's intervention is meant to pull her away from role playing, first on the superficial level of disguises and phony names and later on a deeper psychotherapeutic level. But here, as in the matter of her immobility during the Rutland safe episode, he is drawn into her orbit as much as she is drawn into his: His treatment of her is controlling and manipulative from the beginning, and upon their marriage he becomes another of Hitchcock's on-screen movie directors, guiding her through the wife role with detailed instructions (first you see me to the door, then you give me a kiss . . .) meant to facilitate their joint portrayal of a conventional married couple.

Yet there is more to life in *Marnie,* as in Hitchcock generally, than the surfaces with which such performances are meant to cope. Marnie's relationship with Mark is far more complicated than Melanie's with Mitch, and Hitchcock uses subtle cinematic means to evoke its complexities. One of many examples can be found when Mark kisses Marnie just before their sexual encounter and the camera angle switches from high to low, inscribing a vertical axis that is invisible yet unmistakably phallic in structure, and hence underlines the temporary triumph of Mark's aggressive masculinity over Marnie's troubled and darkly motivated defenses.

A late work chronologically and in tone, *Marnie* echoes themes and tropes from many earlier Hitchcock periods. (An even later film, *Family Plot,* is the all-time champion in this regard, comprising a virtual anthology of allusions to other Hitchcock movies.) Marnie wants to bet on a horse called Telepathy, for instance, suggesting the kind of extrasensory undercurrent that flowed through *Shadow of a Doubt.* The horse's name also provides another thin connection between *Marnie* and *The Birds,* which is based on supernormal events.

Strutt, a pudgy businessman who lusts after the heroine, recalls Cassidy in *Psycho.* What is more interesting, the film has a tendency toward split-screen compositions, which mirror Marnie's fractured psyche while echoing films from *Blackmail* to *Psycho.* As filmmaker Warren Sonbert puts it, "There is a continual emphasis (and contained within the same frame) on the schizophrenic split between images of closure and escape."[2] The major safe-robbing scene is the best example of this, with Marnie on one side of the screen, the empty office — soon invaded by an unexpected outsider — on the other. Hitchcock uses evocative side-by-side compositions on other occasions, too, as after the wedding when Marnie gazes ahead on one side while Mark and Lil kiss on the other, and in a dream sequence when a hand knocks on a window, the rest of the body remaining hidden from view. These are not mere mannerisms of style. The cleaning woman, particularly, has a connection with Marnie that fully warrants her intrusion into a contiguous screen area: While one woman engages in compulsive criminal behavior, the other (looking very much like Marnie's mother) scrubs away at the dirt of human existence, in a scaled-down but chilling allusion to Norman Bates's obsessive clean-up of a far greater crime.

Marnie does not develop its vision of chaos versus order as brilliantly as *The Birds* and *Psycho* develop theirs, and it falls similarly short of other Hitchcock masterpieces. It remains a resonant work, however, with much to reward the receptive spectator — and much to keep Hitchcock champions and detractors engaged in lively, perhaps perpetual debate.

Notes

1. Donald Spoto, *The Dark Side of Genius: The Life of Alfred Hitchcock*. Boston: Little, Brown, 1983. pp. 472–9.
2. Warren Sonbert, "Hitchcock's *Marnie*." Personal communication, 1985.

Select Bibliography

Brill, Lesley, *The Hitchcock Romance: Love and Irony in Hitchcock's Films*. Princeton, N.J.: Princeton University Press, 1988.

Deutelbaum, Marshall, and Leland Poague, eds., *A Hitchcock Reader*. Ames: Iowa State University Press, 1986.

Durgnat, Raymond, *The Strange Case of Alfred Hitchcock, or, the Plain Man's Hitchcock*. Cambridge, Mass: MIT Press, 1974.

LaValley, Albert J., ed., *Focus on Hitchcock*. Englewood Cliffs, N.J.: Prentice-Hall, 1972.

Leff, Leonard J., *Hitchcock and Selznick: The Rich and Strange Collaboration of Alfred Hitchcock and David O. Selznick in Hollywood*. New York: Weidenfeld & Nicolson, 1987.

Modleski, Tania, *The Women Who Knew Too Much: Hitchcock and Feminist Theory*. New York: Methuen, 1988.

Naremore, James, *Filmguide to Psycho*. Bloomington: Indiana University Press, 1973.

Rebello, Stephen, *Alfred Hitchcock and the Making of Psycho*. New York: Dembner, 1990.

Rohmer, Eric, and Claude Chabrol, *Hitchcock: The First Forty-Four Films*, trans. Stanley Hochman. New York: Continuum, 1979.

Rothman, William, *Hitchcock – The Murderous Gaze*. Cambridge, Mass: Harvard University Press, 1982.

Ryall, Tom, *Alfred Hitchcock & the British Cinema*. Urbana: University of Illinois Press, 1986.

Spoto, Donald, *The Dark Side of Genius: The Life of Alfred Hitchcock*. Boston: Little, Brown & Company, 1983.

 The Art of Alfred Hitchcock: Fifty Years of His Motion Pictures. New York: Hopkinson & Blake, 1977.

Truffaut, François, with the collaboration of Helen G. Scott, *Hitchcock*. New York: Simon & Schuster, 1984.

Wood, Robin, *Hitchcock's Films Revisited*. New York: Columbia University Press, 1989.

Filmography

1927

The Pleasure Garden (silent)
Screenplay: Eliot Stannard, after novel by Oliver Sandys
Director of photography: Baron Ventimiglia
Producer/Production company: Michael Balcon, Gainsborough–Emelka, 1925
Cast: Virginia Valli, Carmelita Geraghty, Miles Mander, John Stuart, Nita Naldi, Frederick Martini, Florence Helminger

The Mountain Eagle *(Fear o' God)* (silent)
Screenplay: Eliot Stannard
Director of photography: Baron Ventimiglia
Producer/Production company: Michael Balcon, Gainsborough–Emelka, 1925
Cast: Bernard Goetzke, Nita Naldi, Malcolm Keen, John Hamilton

The Lodger: A Story of the London Fog (silent)
Screenplay: Eliot Stannard, after novel by Marie Belloc Lowndes
Director of photography: Baron Ventimiglia
Editing: Ivor Montagu
Producer/Production company: Michael Balcon, Gainsborough, 1926
Cast: Marie Ault, Arthur Chesney, June, Malcolm Keen, Ivor Novello

Downhill *(When Boys Leave Home)* (silent)
Screenplay: Eliot Stannard, after play by David LeStrange (pseud. Ivor Novello and Constance Collier)
Director of photography: Claude McDonnell
Editing: Ivor Montagu
Producer/Production company: Michael Balcon, Gainsborough
Cast: Ivor Novello, Robin Irvine, Lillian Braithwaite, Isabel Jeans, Ian Hunter

Easy Virtue (silent)
Screenplay: Eliot Stannard, after play by Noël Coward
Director of photography: Claude McDonnell

149

Editing: Ivor Montagu
Producer/Production company: Michael Balcon, Gainsborough
Cast: Isabel Jeans, Franklyn Dyall, Eric Bransby Williams, Ian Hunter, Robin Irvine,
Violet Farebrother

The Ring (silent)
Screenplay: Alfred Hitchcock
Director of photography: John J. Cox
Producer/Production company: John Maxwell, British International
Cast: Carl Brisson, Lillian Hall Davis, Ian Hunter, Harry Terry, Gordon Harker,
Forrester Harvey, Tom Helmore

1928

The Farmer's Wife (silent)
Screenplay: Alfred Hitchcock, after the play by Eden Phillpotts
Director of photography: John J. Cox
Editing: Alfred Booth
Producer/Production company: John Maxwell, British International, 1927
Cast: Jameson Thomas, Lillian Hall Davis, Gordon Harker, Maud Gill, Louise
Pounds, Olga Slade, Antonia Brough

Champagne (silent)
Screenplay: Eliot Stannard
Adaptation: Alfred Hitchcock, after story by Walter C. Mycroft
Director of photography: John J. Cox
Producer/Production company: John Maxwell, British International
Cast: Betty Balfour, Jean Bradin, Theo Von Alten, Gordon Harker

1929

The Manxman (silent)
Screenplay: Eliot Stannard, after novel by Hall Caine
Director of photography: John J. Cox
Producer/Production company: John Maxwell, British International, 1928
Cast: Carl Brisson, Malcolm Keen, Anny Ondra, Randle Ayrton

Blackmail (sound)
Screenplay: Alfred Hitchcock, after play by Charles Bennett
Director of photography: John J. Cox
Editing: Emile de Ruelle
Music: Campbell and Connelly
Producer/Production company: John Maxwell, British International, 1928
Cast: Anny Ondra (voice by Joan Barry), Sara Allgood, Charles Paton, John Long-
den, Donald Calthrop, Cyril Ritchard, Hannah Jones, Phyllis Monkman, Harvey
Braban

Harmony Heaven (silent)
With sequences by: Eddie Pola, Edward Brandt
Production company: British International Pictures, 1929

1930

Juno and the Paycock (sound) [all sound hereafter]
Adaptation: Alfred Hitchcock and Alma Reville, after play by Sean O'Casey
Director of photography: John J. Cox
Producer/Production company: John Maxwell, British International
Cast: Sara Allgood, Edward Chapman, Maire O'Neill, Sidney Morgan

Murder! (German version = *Mary*)
Screenplay: Alma Reville
Adaptation: Alfred Hitchcock and Walter Mycroft, after novel and play *Enter Sir John* by Clemence Dane and Helen Simpson
Director of photography: John J. Cox
Editing: Rene Marrison, Emile de Ruelle
Music: John Reynders
Producer/Production company: John Maxwell, British International
Cast: Norah Baring, Herbert Marshall, Miles Mander, Esme Percy, Edward Chapman, Phyllis Konstam, Hannah Jones, Una O'Connor (German version starred Walter Abel)

Elstree Calling
Codirectors: André Charlot, Jack Hulbert, Paul Murray
Scenario: Val Valentine
Director of photography: Claude Freise Greene
Music: Reg Casson, Vivian Ellis, Chic Endor
Production company: British International Pictures, 1930
Cast: Gordon Harker

1931

The Skin Game
Screenplay: Alma Reville, after play by John Galsworthy
Adaptation: Alfred Hitchcock
Director of photography: John J. Cox
Producer/Production company: John Maxwell, British International, 1930–1
Cast: C. V. France, Helen Haye, Edmund Gwenn, Jill Esmond, John Longden, Phyllis Konstam

1932

Number Seventeen
Screenplay: Alma Reville, Alfred Hitchcock, and Rodney Ackland, after play by J. Jefferson Farjeon

Directors of photography: John J. Cox, Byran Langley
Editing: A. C. Hammond
Music: A. Hallis
Producer/Production company: John Maxwell, British International, 1931
Cast: Leon M. Lion, Anne Grey, John Stuart, Donald Calthrop, Barry Jones, Ann Casson, Henry Caine, Garry Marsh

Rich and Strange *(East of Shanghai)*
Screenplay: Alma Reville
Adaptation: Alfred Hitchcock
Directors of photography: John J. Cox, Charles Martin
Editing: Rene Marrison, Winifred Cooper
Music: Hal Dolphe
Producer/Production company: John Maxwell, British International
Cast: Henry Kendall, Joan Barry, Percy Marmont, Betty Amann, Elsie Randolph

1933

Waltzes from Vienna *(Strauss's Great Waltz)*
Screenplay: Alma Reville, Guy Bolton, after play by Bolton
Music: Johann Strauss
Producer/Production company: Tom Arnold, Tom Arnold Prods.
Cast: Jessie Matthews, Esmond Knight, Edmund Gwenn, Frank Vosper, Fay Compton

1934

The Man Who Knew Too Much
Screenplay: Edwin Greenwood and A. R. Rawlinson, after story by Charles Bennett and D. B. Wyndham Lewis
Director of photography: Curt Courant
Editing: H. St. C. Stewart
Music: Arthur Benjamin
Producer/Production company: Michael Balcon, Gaumont–British
Cast: Leslie Banks, Edna Best, Nova Pilbeam, Peter Lorre, Frank Vosper, Hugh Wakefield, Pierre Fresnay, Cicely Oates, D. A. Clarke Smith, George Curzon

1935

The 39 Steps
Adaptation: Charles Bennett, after novel by John Buchan
Director of photography: Bernard Knowles
Editing: D. N. Twist
Music: Louis Levy
Producer/Production company: Michael Balcon, Gaumont–British
Cast: Robert Donat, Madeleine Carroll, Lucie Mannheim, Godfrey Tearle, John

Laurie, Peggy Ashcroft, Helen Haye, Frank Cellier, Wylie Watson, Gus Mac-Naughton, Jerry Verno, Peggy Simpson

1936

Secret Agent
Screenplay: Charles Bennett, after play by Campbell Dixon (based on stories by W. Somerset Maugham)
Director of photography: Bernard Knowles
Editing: Charles Frend
Music: Louis Levy
Producer/Production company: Michael Balcon, Gaumont–British, 1935
Cast: John Gielgud, Madeleine Carroll, Peter Lorre, Robert Young, Percy Marmont, Florence Kahn, Charles Carson, Lilli Palmer, Michel Saint-Denis

Sabotage *(A Woman Alone)*
Screenplay: Charles Bennett, after novel *The Secret Agent* by Joseph Conrad
Director of photography: Bernard Knowles
Editing: Charles Frend
Music: Louis Levy
Producer/Production company: Michael Balcon, Gaumont–British
Cast: Sylvia Sidney, Oscar Homolka, Desmond Tester, John Loder, Joyce Barbour, William Dewhurst, Martita Hunt, Peter Bull

1938

Young and Innocent *(The Girl Was Young)*
Screenplay: Charles Bennett, Edwin Greenwood, and Anthony Armstrong, after novel *A Shilling for Candles* by Josephine Tey
Director of photography: Bernard Knowles
Editing: Charles Frend
Music: Louis Levy
Producer/Production company: Edward Black, Gaumont–British, 1937
Cast: Nova Pilbeam, Derrick de Marney, Percy Marmont, Edward Rigby, Mary Clare, John Longden, George Curzon, Basil Radford, Pamela Carme

The Lady Vanishes
Screenplay: Sidney Gilliat and Frank Lauder, after novel *The Wheel Spins* by Ethel Lina White
Director of photography: John J. Cox
Editing: R. E. Dearing
Music: Louis Levy
Producer/Production company: Edward Black, Gaumont–British, 1937
Cast: Margaret Lockwood, Michael Redgrave, Dame May Whitty, Paul Lukas, Cecil Parker, Linden Travers, Naunton Wayne, Basil Radford, Mary Clare, Catherine Lacey, Josephine Wilson, Kathleen Tremaine, Emile Boreo, Googie Withers

Jamaica Inn
Screenplay: Sidney Gilliat and Joan Harrison, after novel by Daphne du Maurier
Directors of photography: Harry Stradling, Bernard Knowles
Music: Eric Fenby
Producer/Production company: Erich Pommer, Erich Pommer Prods., 1938
Cast: Charles Laughton, Leslie Banks, Marie Ney, Maureen O'Hara, Emlyn Williams, Wylie Watson, Mervyn Johns, Edwin Greenwood, Stephen Haggard

Rebecca
Screenplay: Robert E. Sherwood and Joan Harrison, after novel by Daphne du Maurier
Adaptation: Philip MacDonald, Michael Hogan
Director of photography: George Barnes
Editing: James Newcom, Hal Kern
Music: Franz Waxman
Producer/Production company: David O. Selznick, Selznick Studios, 1939
Cast: Laurence Olivier, Joan Fontaine, Judith Anderson, George Sanders, Florence Bates, Nigel Bruce, Gladys Cooper, C. Aubrey Smith, Melville Cooper, Leo G. Carroll, Forrester Harvey, Reginald Denny, Lumsden Hare, Philip Winter, Edward Fielding

Foreign Correspondent
Screenplay: Charles Bennet, Joan Harrison
Director of photography: Rudolph Maté
Editing: Otho Lovering, Dorothy Spencer
Music: Alfred Newman
Producer/Production company: Walter Wanger, Wanger Prods.
Cast: Joel McCrea, Laraine Day, Herbert Marshall, George Sanders, Albert Basserman, Robert Benchley, Edmund Gwenn, Harry Davenport, Eduardo Ciannelli, Eddie Conrad, Frances Carson, Martin Kosleck, Gertrude W. Hoffman, Emory Parnell, Ian Wolfe, Eily Malyon, E. E. Clive

Mr. and Mrs. Smith
Story and screenplay: Norman Krasna
Director of photography: Harry Stradling
Editing: William Hamilton
Music: Edward Wand
Producer/Production company: Harry E. Edington, RKO, 1940
Cast: Carole Lombard, Robert Montgomery, Gene Raymond, Philip Merivale, Lucile Watson, Jack Carson

Suspicion
Screenplay: Samson Raphaelson, Joan Harrison, and Alma Reville, after novel *Before the Fact* by Frances Iles
Director of photography: Harry Stradling
Editing: William Hamilton
Music: Franz Waxman
Producer/Production company: Harry E. Edington, RKO
Cast: Joan Fontaine, Cary Grant, Sir Cedric Hardwicke, Dame May Whitty, Nigel Bruce, Isabel Jeans, Heather Angel, Auriol Lee, Leo G. Carroll

1942

Saboteur
Screenplay: Peter Viertel, Joan Harrison, and Dorothy Parker
Director of photography: Joseph Valentine
Editing: Otto Ludwig
Music: Frank Skinner
Producer/Production company: Frank Lloyd, for Universal, 1941
Cast: Robert Cummings, Priscilla Lane, Otto Kruger, Alma Kruger, Norman Lloyd

1943

Shadow of a Doubt
Screenplay: Thornton Wilder, Sally Benson, and Alma Reville, after original story by Gordon McDonnell
Director of photography: Joseph Valentine
Editing: Milton Carruth
Music: Dimitri Tiomkin
Producer/Production company: Jack H. Skirball, for Universal, 1942
Cast: Joseph Cotten, Teresa Wright, MacDonald Carey, Patricia Collinge, Henry Travers, Hume Cronyn, Edna May Wonacott, Charles Bates, Wallace Ford, Eily Malyon, Estelle Jewell

1944

Lifeboat
Screenplay: Jo Swerling, after story by John Steinbeck
Director of photography: Glenn MacWilliams
Editing: Dorothy Spencer
Music: Hugo W. Friedhofer
Producer/Production company: Kenneth Macgowan, 20th Century–Fox, 1943
Cast: Tallulah Bankhead, John Hodiak, William Bendix, Walter Slezak, Mary Anderson, Hume Cronyn, Henry Hull, Heather Angel, Canada Lee

Bon Voyage
Screenplay: J. O. C. Orton, Angus MacPhail, from subject by Arthur Calder-Marshall

Director of photography: Gunther Krampf
Producer/Production company: Sidney Bernstein, British Ministry of Information,
1944
Cast: John Blythe, The Molière Players

Aventure Malgache
Director of photography: Gunther Krampf
Producer/Production company: Sidney Bernstein, British Ministry of Information,
1944
Cast: The Molière Players

1945

Spellbound
Screenplay: Ben Hecht, after novel *The House of Dr. Edwardes* by Francis Beeding
Adaptation: Angus MacPhail
Director of photography: George Barnes
Editing: Hal Kern
Music: Miklos Rozsa
Producer/Production company: David O. Selznick, Selznick Studios, 1944
Cast: Ingrid Bergman, Gregory Peck, Leo G. Carroll, Norman Lloyd, Rhonda Flem-
ing, Michael Chekhov, John Emery, Bill Goodwin, Art Baker, Wallace Ford

1946

Notorious
Screenplay: Ben Hecht
Director of photography: Ted Tetzlaff
Editing: Theron Warth
Music: Roy Webb
Producer/Production company: Alfred Hitchcock, RKO, 1945–6
Cast: Ingrid Bergman, Cary Grant, Claude Rains, Leopoldine Konstantin, Louis
Calhern, Reinhold Schuenzel, Ivan Triesault, Alex Minotis, Eberhard Krumschmidt,
Sir Charles Mendl, Moroni Olsen, Ricardo Costa

1947

The Paradine Case
Screenplay: David O. Selznick, after novel by Robert Hichens
Director of photography: Lee Garmes
Editing: Hal Kern, John Faure
Music: Franz Waxman
Producer/Production company: David O. Selznick, Selznick–Vanguard, 1946–7
Cast: Valli, Gregory Peck, Ann Todd, Charles Laughton, Ethel Barrymore, Charles
Coburn, Joan Tetzel, Louis Jourdan, Leo G. Carroll, John Williams, Isobel Elsom

156

Rope
Screenplay: Arthur Laurents
Adaptation: Hume Cronyn, after play by Patrick Hamilton
Director of photography: Joseph Valentine
Editing: William H. Ziegler
Music: Francis Poulenc, Leo F. Forbstein
Producer/Production company: Alfred Hitchcock and Sidney Bernstein, Transatlantic
Cast: James Stewart, John Dall, Farley Granger, Sir Cedric Hardwicke, Constance Collier, Douglas Dick, Edith Evanson, Joan Chandler, Dick Hogan

1949

Under Capricorn
Screenplay: James Bridie, after play by John Colton and Margaret Linden (based on novel by Helen Simpson)
Adaptation: Hume Cronyn
Director of photography: Jack Cardiff
Editing: A. S. Bates
Music: Richard Addinsell
Producer/Production company: Alfred Hitchcock and Sidney Bernstein, Transatlantic, 1948
Cast: Joseph Cotten, Ingrid Bergman, Michael Wilding, Margaret Leighton, Cecil Parker, Denis O'Dea

1950

Stage Fright
Screenplay: Whitfield Cook, after novel *Man Running* by Selwyn Jepson
Adaptation: Alma Reville
Director of photography: Wilkie Cooper
Editing: E. B. Jarvis
Music: Leighton Lucas
Producer/Production company: Alfred Hitchcock, Warner Bros.–First National, 1949
Cast: Marlene Dietrich, Jane Wyman, Michael Wilding, Richard Todd, Alastair Sim, Sybil Thorndike, Kay Walsh, Patricia Hitchcock, Joyce Grenfell, Miles Malleson, Hector MacGregor, Ballard Berkeley, André Morell

1951

Strangers on a Train
Screenplay: Raymond Chandler and Czenzi Ormonde, after novel by Patricia Highsmith

Adaptation: Whitfield Cook
Director of photography: Robert Burks
Editing: William Ziegler
Music: Dimitri Tiomkin
Producer/Production company: Alfred Hitchcock, Warner Bros.–First National, 1950
Cast: Robert Walker, Farley Granger, Laura Elliott, Ruth Roman, Patricia Hitchcock, Leo G. Carroll, Marion Lorne, Jonathan Hale, Norma Varden

1953

I Confess
Screenplay: George Tabori and William Archibald, after play *Nos Deux consciences* by Paul Anthelme
Director of photography: Robert Burks
Editing: Rudi Fehr
Music: Dimitri Tiomkin
Producer/Production company: Alfred Hitchcock, Warner Bros.–First National, 1952
Cast: Montgomery Clift, Anne Baxter, Karl Malden, Roger Dann, O. E. Hasse, Dolly Haas, Brian Aherne

1954

Dial "M" for Murder
Screenplay: Frederick Knott, after his play
Director of photography: Robert Burks (shot in 3-D)
Editing: Rudi Fehr
Music: Dimitri Tiomkin
Producer/Production company: Alfred Hitchcock, Warner Bros.–First National, 1952
Cast: Ray Milland, Grace Kelly, Robert Cummings, Anthony Dawson, John Williams, Leo Britt, Patrick Allen, George Alderson, Robin Hughes

Rear Window
Screenplay: John Michael Hayes, after story by Cornell Woolrich
Director of photography: Robert Burks
Editing: George Tomasini
Music: Franz Waxman
Producer/Production company: Alfred Hitchcock, Paramount, 1953
Cast: James Stewart, Grace Kelly, Thelma Ritter, Wendell Corey, Raymond Burr, Irene Winston, Judith Evelyn, Ross Bagdasarian, Georgine Darcy, Jesslyn Fax, Sara Berner, Frank Cady, Rand Harper, Havis Davenport, Anthony Ward

1955

To Catch a Thief
Screenplay: John Michael Hayes, after novel by David Dodge
Director of photography: Robert Burks

Editing: George Tomasini
Music: Lyn Murray
Producer/Production company: Alfred Hitchcock, Paramount, 1954
Cast: Cary Grant, Grace Kelly, Jessie Royce Landis, John Williams, Brigitte Auber, Charles Vanel, René Blanchard

The Trouble with Harry
Screenplay: John Michael Hayes, after novel by J. Trevor Story
Director of photography: Robert Burks
Editing: Alma Macrorie
Music: Bernard Herrmann
Producer/Production company: Alfred Hitchcock, Paramount, 1954
Cast: Edmund Gwenn, John Forsythe, Shirley MacLaine, Mildred Natwick, Mildred Dunnock, Jerry Mathers, Royal Dano, Parker Fennelly, Philip Truex

Films made for TV: *Breakdown, Revenge, The Case of Mr. Pelham*

1956

The Man Who Knew Too Much
Screenplay: John Michael Hayes, after story by Charles Bennett and D. B. Wyndham Lewis
Director of photography: Robert Burks
Editing: George Tomasini
Music: Bernard Herrmann
Producer/Production company: Alfred Hitchcock, Paramount, 1955
Cast: James Stewart, Doris Day, Christopher Olsen, Bernard Miles, Brenda de Banzie, Reggie Nalder, Daniel Gélin, Ralph Truman, Mogens Wieth, Hilary Brooke, Carolyn Jones, Alan Mowbray, Richard Wattis, Alix Talton

The Wrong Man
Screenplay: Maxwell Anderson and Angus MacPhail, after story by Anderson
Director of photography: Robert Burks
Editing: George Tomasini
Music: Bernard Herrmann
Producer/Production company: Alfred Hitchcock, Warner Bros.–First National
Cast: Henry Fonda, Vera Miles, Anthony Quayle, Esther Minciotti, Harold J. Stone, John Heldabrand, Doreen Lang, Laurinda Barrett, Norma Connolly, Lola D'Annunzio, Nehemiah Persoff, Robert Essen, Kippy Campbell, Dayton Lummia, Charles Cooper, Peggy Webber, Richard Robbins

Films made for TV: *Back for Christmas, Wet Saturday, Mr. Blanchard's Secret*

1957

Films made for TV: *One More Mile to Go, The Perfect Crime, Four O'Clock*

Vertigo
Screenplay: Alec Coppel and Samuel Taylor, after novel *D'Entre les morts* by Pierre Boileau and Thomas Narcejac
Director of photography: Robert Burks
Editing: George Tomasini
Music: Bernard Herrmann
Producer/Production company: Alfred Hitchcock, Paramount, 1957
Cast: James Stewart, Kim Novak, Barbara Bel Geddes, Tom Helmore, Konstantin Shayne, Henry Jones, Raymond Bailey, Ellen Corby, Lee Patrick

Films made for TV: *Lamb to the Slaughter, Dip in the Pool, Poison*

1959

North by Northwest
Screenplay: Ernest Lehman
Director of photography: Robert Burks
Editing: George Tomasini
Music: Bernard Herrmann
Producer/Production company: Alfred Hitchcock, MGM, 1958
Cast: Cary Grant, Eva Marie Saint, James Mason, Jessie Royce Landis, Leo G. Carroll, Philip Ober, Martin Landau, Adam Williams, Robert Ellenstein, Josephine Hutchinson, Doreen Lang, Les Tremayne, Philip Coolidge, Edward Binns, Pat McVey, Nora Marlowe, Ned Glass, Malcolm Atterbury

Films made for TV: *Banquo's Chair, Arthur, The Crystal Trench*

1960

Psycho
Screenplay: Joseph Stefano, after novel by Robert Bloch
Director of photography: John L. Russell
Editing: George Tomasini
Music: Bernard Herrmann
Producer/Production company: Alfred Hitchcock, Paramount, 1959–60
Cast: Anthony Perkins, Janet Leigh, Vera Miles, John Gavin, Martin Balsam, John McIntire, Lurene Tuttle, Simon Oakland, Frank Albertson, Patricia Hitchcock, Vaughn Taylor, Mort Mills, John Anderson

Films made for TV: *Incident at a Corner, Mrs. Bixby and the Colonel's Coat*

1961

Films made for TV: *The Horseplayer, Bang! You're Dead*

Film made for TV: *I Saw the Whole Thing*

The Birds
Screenplay: Evan Hunter, after story by Daphne du Maurier
Director of photography: Robert Burks
Editing: George Tomasini
Music: Remi Gassmann, Oskar Sala, Bernard Herrmann
Producer/Production company: Alfred Hitchcock, Universal, 1962
Cast: Tippi Hedren, Rod Taylor, Jessica Tandy, Suzanne Pleshette, Veronica Cartwright, Ethel Griffies, Charles McGraw, Ruth McDevitt, Malcolm Atterbury, Lonny Chapman, Elizabeth Wilson, Jow Mantell, Doodles Weaver, John McGovern, Karl Swenson, Richard Deacon, Doreen Lang

Marnie
Screenplay: Jay Presson Allen, after novel by Winston Graham
Director of photography: Robert Burks
Editing: George Tomasini
Music: Bernard Herrmann
Producer/Production company: Alfred Hitchcock, Universal, 1963-4
Cast: Tippi Hedren, Sean Connery, Diane Baker, Louise Latham, Martin Gabel, Bob Sweeney, Alan Napier, Mariette Hartley, Edith Evanson, S. John Launer, Meg Wyllie, Bruce Dern

Torn Curtain
Screenplay: Brian Moore
Director of photography: John F. Warren
Editing: Bud Hoffman
Music: John Addison
Producer/Production company: Alfred Hitchcock, Universal, 1965-6
Cast: Paul Newman, Julie Andrews, Lila Kedrova, Wolfgang Kieling, Tamara Toumanova, Ludwig Donath, David Opatoshu, Mort Mills, Carolyn Conwell, Arthur Gould-Porter, Gloria Gorvin

Topaz
Screenplay: Samuel Taylor, after novel by Leon Uris
Director of photography: Jack Hildyard
Editing: William Ziegler

Music: Maurice Jarre
Producer/Production company: Alfred Hitchcock, Universal, 1968–9
Cast: Frederick Stafford, John Forsythe, Dany Robin, John Vernon, Karin Dor, Michel Piccoli, Philippe Noiret, Claude Jade, Roscoe Lee Browne, Per-Axel Arosenius, Michel Subor

1972

Frenzy
Screenplay: Anthony Shaffer, after novel *Goodbye Picadilly, Farewell Leicester Square* by Arthur La Bern
Director of photography: Gil Taylor
Editing: John Jympson
Music: Ron Goodwin
Producer/Production company: Alfred Hitchcock, Universal, 1971
Cast: Jon Finch, Barry Foster, Barbara Leigh-Hunt, Anna Massey, Alex McCowen, Vivien Merchant, Billie Whitelaw, Clive Swift, Bernard Bribbins, Elsie Randolph, Michael Bates, Jean Marsh

1976

Family Plot
Screenplay: Ernest Lehman, after novel *The Rainbird Pattern* by Victor Canning
Director of photography: Leonard South
Editing: J. Terry Williams
Music: John Williams
Producer/Production company: Alfred Hitchcock, Universal, 1965
Cast: Karen Black, Bruce Dern, Barbara Harris, William Devane, Ed Lauter, Cathleen Nesbitt, Katherine Helmond, Warren J. Kemmerling, Edith Atwater, William Prince, Nicolas Colasanto, Marge Redmond

Additional films cited

Battleship Potemkin (Bronenosets Potemkin), dir. Sergei Eisenstein (USSR, 1925)

Citizen Kane, dir. Orson Welles (RKO, U.S., 1941)

Gaslight, dir. George Cukor (MGM, U.S., 1944)

Nosferatu, a Symphony of Horror (Nosferatu – Eine Symphonie des Grauens), dir. F. W. Murnau (Germany, 1922)

Lady from Shanghai, The, dir. Orson Welles (Columbia, U.S., 1948)

Seventh Heaven, dir. Frank Borzage (Fox, U.S., 1927)

Stranger, The, dir. Orson Welles (International Pictures/RKO, U.S., 1946)

Touch of Evil, dir. Orson Welles (Universal–International, U.S., 1958)

Index